IF I PERISH
I PERISH

IF I PERISH I PERISH

by

MAJOR W. IAN THOMAS

ZONDERVAN
PUBLISHING HOUSE

OF THE ZONDERVAN CORPORATION
GRAND RAPIDS, MICHIGAN 49506

Dedicated to Timothy Andrew, my youngest son and the latest member of the Team, with the earnest prayer that when he grows up, he may love Jesus Christ with all his heart, and become expendable for God.

Foreword

The response to the writings of Major W. Ian Thomas has been unusually warm and spontaneous. On both sides of the Atlantic, all across the United States, and, indeed, around the world, readers have welcomed his unique approach to Bible exposition and his insight-filled presentation of Biblical truth. Wherever his books have reached in their world-wide ministry, they have won for him devoted followers.

This newest release, *If I Perish, I Perish,* is as refreshingly different and contemporary as his previous works. His is not the usual hackneyed and sometimes prosaic approach to the Old Testament so commonly produced. Instead, this allegorical expression of truth in the Christian life is unforgettable in its impact, striking in its unique development of theme and purpose. The Book of Esther takes on new meaning and significance under Major Thomas' authoritative pen.

THE PUBLISHERS

CONTENTS

1

Which Things Are an Allegory

I'M TIRED OF RELIGION — AND TO BE ENTIRELY HONEST I know of nothing quite so boring as Christianity without Christ.

Have you ever tried to start a car without fuel, until there wasn't a spark left in the battery? Then you will know exactly what I mean, for there are few things more frustrating than a car that will not go. Everything is nicely greased and in its rightful place, and all the working parts move dutifully, but try as you may, there isn't the suspicion of a kick, nor the tiniest evidence of life in the engine. You might just as well dump the thing, for all the chance you have of getting it on the move!

Countless people have stopped going to a place of worship simply because they are sick of going through the motions of a dead religion. They are tired of trying to start a car on an empty tank!

What a pity it is that there are not a few more people around to tell them that Jesus Christ is alive. I spoke of nothing more boring than Christianity without Christ, but I know of nothing so utterly exciting as being a Christian — sharing the very life of Jesus

Christ on earth right here and now, and being caught up with Him into the relentless, invincible purposes of an almighty God, and with all the limitless resources of deity available for the job.

Can you imagine anything more exciting than that?

Do you know what it is to live purposefully? Is there an urgent sense of mission or some compelling thrust within you which makes life add up to the sheer adventure that God always intended life to be? Or are you simply engaged in the struggle for existence and survival?

Worse still, far from being caught up into the invincible purposes of an almighty God, have you been caught up into the rat race of competitive existence? haunted by the fear of being overtaken on the bend? breathlessly trying to keep abreast of events that travel faster than your capacity to cope with them?

If so, I think you will be interested in the following extracts from a letter I received several years ago from a student attending Bible College.

"I am writing to thank you for your six devotional lectures, the effect of which upon my life, it would be difficult to exaggerate. I have been a Christian for four years, but I came home feeling like a person who has just discovered that he has passed the last four years sitting unwittingly on a million pounds—only the riches I have discovered cannot justly be compared to that sort of treasure."

That is how the letter began, and I would like to share with you a little more of what he had to say.

"I believe that God prepared me for those lectures: last term I had to prepare a talk on 'I am . . . the Truth'

(John 14:6). One of the two main headings under which I was collecting and jotting down my thoughts was 'Jesus is the Truth.' The fundamental characteristic of truth is consistency: it must fit every known and unknown fact and situation, and is absolute.

"I get the picture in my mind of a giant jigsaw puzzle: if I have anything but the truth, at least one of the pieces will not fit and others will need forcing into place. The fundamental idea behind 'Jesus is the Truth' was that Jesus is the key to the understanding of all things, and almost the first thing you said **was** that the Lord Jesus Christ *is* the final exegesis of **all** things. Thus God prepared my mind.

"As I listened, as I copied up my notes and as ever since I have read my Bible and thought about it, pieces of the jigsaw puzzle have been falling over each other in their eagerness to tumble into place!

"It is as if I had been collecting pieces for the past four years but just flinging them into the box without any real thought of fitting them together. Now each time I come across one of these pieces it seems to fit into the total scheme of spiritual life and into the whole scheme of things in general, from verses of Scripture to insignificant things of everyday experience.

"I find it difficult to describe this sense of being utterly at one and in harmony with the Lord Jesus. Spiritual wisdom has become part of the sum total of experience rather than something detached and fragmental.

"My life since my conversion has been one of striving to work *for* Christ instead of letting Him work *through* me. What a difference there is now that HE and not work for Him, has the pre-eminence.

"Now I really realise that not only am I in Christ but that Christ is in me — I also realise that there is no further basic issue to face! Humanly speaking those six lectures have helped me more than all the talks, lectures, sermons, books and examples which I have experienced since my conversion.

"The Lord Jesus said: 'I am come that they might have life, and that they might have it more abundantly.' I now know what He meant — because I have it!"

The writer of this letter is now a pilot with the Missionary Aviation Fellowship in Ethiopia and quite recently flew me over the mountains into Addis Ababa. It was thrilling to discover that the intervening years had served only to establish ever more firmly in his own experience, the principles of true discipleship which he had so readily embraced.

Trading his poverty for Christ's wealth and his weakness for Christ's strength, this young man has exchanged the bankruptcy of the fallen Adam for all the fullness of the life of Christ, and has discovered the sheer adventure of allowing Jesus Christ to be God in his own experience — for God He is!

I wonder whether you have learned to do the same? To detach your Christianity from Christ is to reduce it to the impotence of a dead religion, impersonal to Him and impersonal to you — just an intellectual exercise or a sentimental formula — and Christianity is neither.

Christianity is Christ — it involves a principle of life which pulsates with divine energy and cannot be explained apart from God Himself. It is essentially miraculous even though it does not have to be sensational. It is always supernatural, in that it lies beyond the scope of mortal man apart from the indwelling presence of the risen Son of God.

It is with the object of making the same wonderful discovery, that we are about to embark together upon this series of studies in the Book of Esther.

You may be somewhat surprised at my choice of the Book of Esther for this particular purpose, but I know of no other single book in the whole of the Old Testament which more lucidly illustrates the principles governing the Christian life. Nor is there a book which demonstrates more clearly what spiritual new birth really involves and what conditions must be met, to be filled with the Holy Spirit and to become effective for God.

Within the pages of the Book of Esther there is to be found a wealth of understanding concerning the implications of true discipleship, and concerning that relentless war for final supremacy being waged within the soul of man between good and evil — between God and the devil. It is fascinating beyond description to find, with the unfolding of the story, so meticulous an explanation of so much that often baffles the honest but hard-pressed believer.

If you are genuinely concerned to find the key to victorious living and to that dimension of spiritual experience that makes you "more than conqueror" — then read on and join me in this exploration.

Before we begin to examine the story I would like to say a word concerning Bible exegesis, or exposition, which I trust may be helpful to all and especially to those whose responsibility it is to take the Word of God and unfold its message to others.

It is important to bear in mind that the whole Bible, throughout both Old and New Testaments, is a total revelation authored by the Holy Spirit, and that no part may be detached from the rest nor be incompatible to the truth as consistently revealed throughout the whole of Scripture.

In the fourth chapter of his epistle to the Galatians, and with reference to the birth of Isaac and Ishmael, Paul writes in the twenty-fourth verse, "which things are an allegory." The Apostle clearly recognizes that behind the historical events there is a unique symbolism by which the Holy Spirit has chosen to illustrate in the Old Testament spiritual truth enunciated in the New Testament. It is a correct understanding of this hidden symbolism which offers to us the key to correct spiritualization, which in turn provides the basis for accurate Biblical illustration.

Correct spiritualization provides the expositional constants to which all Biblical illustration must be true, if it is to be accurate and safe, for these constants involve principles which may never be violated.

Allow me to explain to you what I mean by an expositional constant. The Holy Spirit as Author of the Bible has chosen particular people, nations, countries, animals or inanimate objects as symbols with which to convey certain different spiritual meanings. Once you have learned the language of the Holy Spirit and recognize one of these symbols in any particular portion of the Bible, you will be alerted to the fact that He is making reference to that which is represented by the particular symbol which He is using.

It is the spiritual significance of these symbols which I have described above as a "spiritual constant," because of the relentless consistency with which the Holy Spirit uses these symbols throughout the whole of the Bible. One such which readily comes to mind is oil, which in both Old and New Testaments always represents the person, office and work of the Holy Spirit Himself, as indeed do wind and fire.

Another which I am sure you will recognize at once as being equally obvious is the snake or serpent, used by the Holy Spirit to represent Satan, or the sin that has its origin in Satan. The devil is pictured as a serpent in the record of man's fall into sin (Genesis 3:1), and is directly referred to in this way in the twelfth and twentieth chapters of the Revelation, ". . . that old serpent, which is the devil." Paul was certainly in no doubt as to whom he was referring in II Corinthians 11:3 —

> "But I fear, lest by any means, as the serpent beguiled Eve through his subtilty, so your minds should be corrupted from the simplicity that is in Christ."

The Lord Jesus Christ spoke of the Pharisees as "a generation of vipers," having told them plainly — "Ye are of your father the devil, and the lusts of your father ye will do" (John 8:44).

An allegory is the describing of a subject under the guise of another which resembles and suggests it, as of course was the case in the use made by the Lord

Jesus of parables. By this means He clarified the truth which He wished to communicate, underlined it and impressed it upon His hearers. Another example of an allegory in more recent time is Bunyan's *Pilgrim's Progress* or his *Holy War*, and of still more recent authorship, *The Screwtape Letters*, by C. S. Lewis.

I would like to make it clear to you therefore at the outset of our journey together, that although there is in my mind absolutely no doubt as to the historical accuracy or divine authorship of the Book of Esther, I shall be using the story as an allegory to clarify and illustrate spiritual truths soundly established and substantiated elsewhere in the Bible, and all of which must be entirely compatible with the total revelation given to us by the Holy Spirit in the whole of the Scriptures.

This being so, I need hardly say that I do not claim any monopoly whatsoever in the interpretation of the Book of Esther, but simply add these thoughts to the countless others which have already been legitimately expressed, with the earnest prayer that God may be pleased to own them and to honor them in the hearts of my readers and that as one such, you personally may be enriched and encouraged in your knowledge of our wonderful Lord Jesus Christ and that in consequence, He for His part may be allowed to enter ever more fully into His inheritance in your life.

2

Haman the Agagite —
Murder in the Making!

IT MIGHT NOT SEEM TO YOU ENTIRELY LOGICAL, BUT
I would like you to begin with me at chapter three in
the Book of Esther, for in the first two verses we are
introduced to three characters all of whom play a sig-
nificant role in the unfolding of the story.

> "After these things did king Ahasuerus promote
> Haman the son of Hammedatha the Agagite, and
> advanced him, and set his seat above all the princes
> that were with him.
> "And all the king's servants, that were in the
> king's gate, bowed, and reverenced Haman: for the
> king had so commanded concerning him. But Mor-
> decai bowed not, nor did him reverence."

King Ahasuerus reigned, we are told in chapter
one verse one, "From India unto Ethiopia, over an hundred and seven and twenty provinces," and may well
be identified with the better known King Xerxes, who
reigned from 486 to 465 B.C. The *Zondervan Pictorial
Bible Dictionary* gives four close similarities between
them which support this identification, and in the same

volume it is noted that in all probability the Ahasuerus
of Ezra 4:6 is also the same person.

As the king in his palace, Ahasuerus will represent
for us the soul of man, for it was within the palace that
decisions were made, policies declared, and decrees
published.

The kingdom of one hundred and twenty-seven
provinces will represent the human body, for throughout the length and breadth of the land the laws promul-
gated in the palace had their repercussions, being communicated in this way to the outside world. From the
largest city to the tiniest village the conduct of the
people and the way they behaved was affected by the
king's commands.

It is within the soul that human behavior is determined, for it is within the soul that decisions are made,
plans conceived and the will exercised to bring the
body into action. In this way the thoughts and the in-
tents of the heart may be communicated to the outside
world in terms of human behavior.

I have dealt more fully with the function of the
soul as the seat of human behavior in *The Mystery of
Godliness* in the chapter entitled "The Nature of a
Man," but it is necessary here to remind you that the
will is exercised under the influence of the mind and
the emotions. Whatever influence it may be that controls the mind and the emotions will ultimately control
the will, and this fact leads us to consider the role of
Haman the Agagite in the story recorded in the Book
of Esther.

Haman the Agagite will represent what in the New
Testament is called the flesh; not of course the human

body, but that perverted principle which perpetuates in man Satan's proud hostility and enmity against God.

You will notice that from the outset of the story Haman is already deeply entrenched within the palace, firmly established in the king's affections and enjoying his complete confidence, for he "advanced him, and set his seat above all the princes that were with him." In his presence, as an act of reverence, every head had to bow.

Haman from within the palace had constant, unhindered access to the king, and in his own subtle way colored the king's thinking, stirred the king's emotions, and with his malicious evil influence moulded the king's decisions, so that by every royal decree to the very extremities of the kingdom, the character of this wicked man made its impact upon the nation.

On the other hand, sitting in the king's gate outside the palace and having no access to the king, and exercising no influence whatsoever over him, was one who refused to bow in the presence of Haman — his name was Mordecai.

Mordecai will represent the Person of the Holy Spirit, of whose presence the unregenerate soul is destitute — and you and I were born in this unregenerate condition. The Holy Spirit is the inveterate foe of the flesh — "For the flesh lusteth against the Spirit, and the Spirit against the flesh: and these are contrary the one to the other" (Galatians 5:17).

No doubt by now you are beginning to get the picture. Here is man in his fallen condition, his soul dominated by the flesh and destitute of the Holy Spirit, just as the king was dominated by Haman and deprived of the counsel of Mordecai. Man's humanity is prostituted by Satan and deprived of those gracious and benevolent influences of the Spirit of Christ, by whose indwelling it was God's original intention that man should share His life, and become by creation a partaker of the divine nature.

The story begins with the *wrong man* in and the *right man* out, and the problem to be resolved becomes quite obviously apparent — how to get the wrong man *out* and the right man *in!* This is what the Gospel is all about.

Quite obviously, to get the wrong man out and the right man in, and thus to exchange the malicious, evil influence of Haman for the gracious, benevolent influence of Mordecai, is going to involve an entirely new situation within the palace and a radical change of government. Needless to say, such a change of government within the palace is going to have far reaching consequences throughout the kingdom. No one will be left in any doubt as to what has really happened.

In the spiritual sense, nothing less than this will be involved if in becoming a Christian it is your desire to *be* the Christian you have *become.*

AMALEK AT IT AGAIN!

You may wonder why I seem to be gunning for Haman, and may ask "Why have you got your knife into him? What has Haman done to deserve it, and what reasonable excuse do you have for painting such a sinister picture of the man?"

Maybe you even feel a little sympathy for Haman and think that it is presumption on my part to blacken his character without ever having put him on trial. Allow me to disillusion you, gentle friend, if out of charity you feel inclined to champion his cause!

Haman is full of hate, and hidden in his heart beneath the veneer of disarming charm there is murder in the making. His ways are the ways of death! It is in the person of Haman that we are alerted by the Holy Spirit to the main thrust of the book, for if we examine his pedigree, we discover in Haman one of those exposirional constants to which I have already made reference in the preceding chapter.

Haman did not like the Jews!

This is a fact which we may readily ascertain from the most casual reading of the text.

> "And the king took his ring from his hand, and gave it unto Haman the son of Hammedatha the Agagite, the Jews' enemy" (3:10).

> "On that day did the king Ahasuerus give the house of Haman the Jews' enemy unto Esther the queen" (8:1).

> "The ten sons of Haman the son of Hammedatha, the enemy of the Jews, slew they; but on the spoil laid they not their hand" (9:10).

> "Because Haman the son of Hammedatha, the Agagite, the enemy of all the Jews, had devised against the Jews to destroy them . . . (9:24).

Why did Haman hate the Jews? Did he not like the look of their faces, or was there a deeper significance to this murderous hostility, in which was to be conceived the bloodthirsty plan "to destroy, to kill, and to cause to perish, all Jews, both young and old, little children and women, in one day, even upon the thirteenth day of the twelfth month, which is the month Adar, to take the spoil of them for a prey"? (3:13).

In my book *The Saving Life of Christ* I have devoted two chapters to the study of Amalek, grandson of Esau and father of the Amalekites with whom God had declared Himself to be at war from generation to generation. If you have not already had occasion. to read *The Saving Life of Christ*, please forgive my boldness in suggesting that you take the earliest opportunity of doing so, for its contents, especially in reference to Amalek, have a strong bearing upon the spiritual content of the Book of Esther.

Suffice it, however, for the moment, that we might get the sense of the matter, to make this quotation,

> "In Esau the spirit of Satan was incarnate. 'What do I need of a birthright restoring me to dependence upon God? I am independent, and I am self-sufficient, and I will be what I am, by virtue of what I am!'"

> "Why did God hate Esau? Because God can do absolutely nothing with a man who will not admit that he needs anything from God. Esau rejected God's means of grace, he repudiated man's need of God's intervention, he *despised his birthright* — and God never forgave him! This is the basic attitude of sin — it makes God irrelevant to the stern business of living, and gives to man a flattering sense of self-importance.

> "God can do nothing for the man eaten up with the spirit of Esau.

> "Amalek was Esau's grandson! And Malachi tells us that the descendants of Esau were a 'people

against whom the Lord hath indigation for ever'
(Malachi 1:4), and Exodus 17 tells us that God was
at war with Amalek from generation to generation.
Perpetuated in Amalek was the profanity of Esau,
the man who refused the birthright.

"There was no good thing in Amalek! There was
absolutely no salvageable content in Amalek! There
was nothing in Amalek upon which God would
look with favor. That was God's mind, God's will,
and God's judgment concerning Amalek.

"But Saul forgot to remember!

"Though he smote the Amalekites, Saul '. . . took
Agag the king of the Amalekites alive' — a king of
Edom, whom God had sentenced to death! . . . Saul
presumed to find something good in what God had
condemned. This was the sin of Saul. He kept the
best of what God had hated!"[1]

So Agag was an Edomite, a descendant of Esau,
the despiser of the birthright — and Agag was the king
of the Amalekites, thus Haman was also an Amalekite,
for Haman was an Agagite (Esther 3:1) and the Amalekites were the inveterate enemies of Israel.

In the person of Haman, descendant of Agag, king
of the Amalekites — Amalekite was at it again!

As Satan hated God, so Cain had hated Abel, and
Ishmael hated Isaac; and as Ishmael hated Isaac so
Esau hated Jacob and Amalek hated Israel; and as
Amalek hated Israel, so Haman hated the Jew!

In this connection it is interesting to note that
Herod the Great, who, in his attempt to kill the Lord
Jesus, ordered the destruction of all the children in

[1] *The Saving Life of Christ* (Zondervan: Grand Rapids, 1961), pp. 93,
94, 99, 108.

Bethlehem two years of age and under, was an Edomite. According to John Peter Lange's commentary on Matthew, Herod the Great was the first sovereign of the Idumaean race of Edomites, which from the year forty before Christ, reigned over Jerusalem under the supremacy of Rome. Herod was an Amalekite, descendant of Esau and of the kith and kin of Haman.

In this commentary on Matthew's gospel it is stated, and I quote from page sixty — "In the design of Herod the old enmity of Edom against Jacob seems to reappear. We are involuntarily reminded of that murderous purpose, 'I will slay my brother Jacob' (Genesis 27:41), which Esau relinquished in his own person, but bequeathed to his posterity."[2]

Haman was true to his breed, and within his wicked heart there seethed this inherent enmity against the Promised Seed, for God had promised — ". . . there shall come a Star out of Jacob, and a Sceptre shall arise out of Israel . . . Out of Jacob shall come he that shall have dominion" (Numbers 24:17, 19).

Haman was a ready tool in the hands of the devil in the pursuit of Satan's vicious ambition to thwart God's redemptive and regenerative purpose — that of re-establishing His divine sovereignty within the soul of man.

Here, indeed, was murder in the making!

---

[2] *Lange's Commentary on the Holy Scriptures*, Vol. 8 (Zondervan: Grand Rapids, 1960), p. 60.

3

City Perplexed—
The Holy Spirit Resisted

IF THERE WAS ONE THING MORE THAN ANOTHER WHICH made Haman livid, it was the fact that in the king's gate there was one who looked him straight in the eyes with cold contempt, and whose head was never bowed in his presence.

> "Then the king's servants, which were in the king's gate, said unto Mordecai, Why transgressest thou the king's commandment?
>
> "Now it came to pass, when they spake daily unto him, and he hearkened not unto them, that they told Haman, to see whether Mordecai's matters would stand: for he told them that he was a Jew.
>
> "And when Haman saw that Mordecai bowed not, nor did him reverence, then was Haman full of wrath" (3:3-5).

Haman recognized in Mordecai his archenemy, for in him he saw the ultimate of all that which elicited his hatred for the Jew.

There is something frighteningly authoritative about the look of quiet, unflinching confidence upon the face of a man who knows that he is right, and at peace with God. The high priest and the council discovered this when, looking steadfastly on Stephen, they "saw his face as it had been the face of an angel," and heard him denounce their guilt without any suggestion of apology nor hint of fear, in words which cut them to the heart — "Ye stiffnecked and uncircumcised in heart and ears, ye do always resist the Holy Ghost: as your fathers did, so do ye." And they gnashed on him with their teeth!

It was the look upon the face of the Lord Jesus Christ which, perhaps more than anything else, frightened Herod and Pontius Pilate on that day when they both washed their hands of Him and were made friends together. A bad conscience is always uneasy in the presence of truth, and whether it be in the presence of Mordecai, or Stephen or the Lord Jesus Christ Himself, it cries out hysterically — "Hang him! Stone him! Crucify Him!"

You may shoot truth between the eyes when it looks you quietly in the face, but it will not be truth which falls victim to your bullet. It was not truth that lay bleeding, dying on a stony slope on the day that Stephen was stoned to death; nor was it truth that hung upon a cross to be buried in a tomb — sin was there condemned and Satan judged!

> "For what the law could not do, in that it was weak through the flesh, God sending his own Son in the likeness of sinful flesh, and for sin, condemned sin in the flesh;
> "That the righteousness of the law might be fulfilled in us, who walk not after the flesh, but after the Spirit" (Romans 8:3, 4).

On the third morning truth was vindicated — *gospel* truth — and Jesus Christ was declared to be the Son of

God with power by His Resurrection from the dead (Romans 1:4). The Son of God, who came into this world to get the wrong man out by taking the flesh into the place of death upon the cross, and to get the Right Man in by the gift of the Holy Spirit to those who claim redemption through His blood, He is the Truth — the Truth that sets men free!

Haman saw in the Jews a threat to his authority, a threat personified in the unbending defiance of Mordecai.

> "And he thought scorn to lay hands on Mordecai alone; for they had shewed him the people of Mordecai: wherefore Haman sought to destroy all the Jews that were throughout the whole kingdom of Ahasuerus, even the people of Mordecai.
>
> "And Haman said unto king Ahasuerus, There is a certain people scattered abroad and dispersed among the people in all the provinces of thy kingdom; and their laws are diverse from all people; neither keep they the king's laws: therefore it is not for the king's profit to suffer them.
>
> "If it please the king, let it be written that they may be destroyed: and I will pay ten thousand talents of silver to the hands of those that have the charge of the business, to bring it into the king's treasuries" (3:6, 8, 9).

Haman recognized that laws had been entrusted to the Jews which, were they to be imposed upon the land, would involve a radical change of government and introduce an entirely new way of life which would be incompatible with that which derived from his own evil influence. It was this that had to be resisted at all costs.

Whose then were these laws entrusted to the Jews,
to which Haman took such strong exception? They
were the oracles of God and represented that true spiritual content of the Jewish nation of which, as a people,
the Jews gave but feeble expression.

> "For he is not a Jew, which is one outwardly;
> neither is that circumcision, which is outward in the
> flesh:
> "But he is a Jew, which is one inwardly; and cir-
> cumcision is that of the heart, in the spirit, and not
> in the letter; whose praise is not of men, but of God.
> "What advantage then hath the Jew? or what
> profit is there of circumcision?
> "Much every way: chiefly, because that unto
> them were committed the oracles of God" (Romans
> 2:28, 29; 3:1, 2).

> "He declares His Word to Jacob, His statutes and
> His ordinances to Israel.
> "He has not dealt so with any (other) nation"
> (Psalm 147:19, 20, *Amplified Bible*).

Don't forget that in the unfolding of the story of
the Book of Esther, Haman represents for us the flesh
and Mordecai the Holy Spirit, and we understand from
the epistle to the Romans that "they that are after the
flesh do mind the things of the flesh: but they that are
after the Spirit, the things of the Spirit." So we may
interpret Paul's words to the Roman Christians this
way:

> "For to be carnally minded (*Haman minded*) is
> death: but to be spiritually minded (*Mordecai
> minded*) is life and peace.
> "Because the carnal mind (*the Haman mind*) is

enmity against God: for it is not subject to the law of God, neither indeed can be" (Romans 8:5-7).

Being hostile to God Himself, it follows that the flesh is hostile to the law of God, and any steps which God might take to re-establish His law in the heart of man will be resisted tooth and nail. Being already entrenched within the human soul by nature, as Haman was already entrenched within the palace of the king, the flesh is in an admirable position to incite the mind, the emotions and the will of unregenerate man to defy God, resist His grace, and keep the Right Man out.

It was to this end that Haman approached King Ahasuerus (representing the human soul) and persuaded him with his subtilty that the introduction of the divine law into the affairs of the kingdom could only be to the detriment of the king's best interests, and that the voice therefore of this people, the Jews, who represented that law, must be ruthlessly silenced. This is a lie which continues to be propagated by Satan today with signal success in the hearts of countless men and women and boys and girls, who have allowed themselves to be persuaded that to give themselves back to the God who made them, and to submit themselves to His sovereignty, is to be robbed of that liberty which makes life really worth living.

Such people are not necessarily insincere in this conviction, but are the victims of their own ignorance, which makes them dupes of the devil whose chiefest delight it is to exploit that ignorance.

"Their moral understanding is darkened and their reasoning is beclouded. [They are] alienated, (estranged, self-banished) from the life of God — with no share in it. [This is] because of the ignorance — the want of knowledge and perception, the willful blindness — that is deep-seated in them, due to their hardness of heart (to the insensitiveness of their moral nature" (Ephesians 4:18, *Amplified Bible*).

"For the god of this world has blinded the unbelievers' minds (that they should not discern the truth), preventing them from seeing the illuminating light of the Gospel of the glory of Christ, the Messiah, Who is the image *and* likeness of God" (II Corinthians 4:4, *Amplified Bible*).

It is for this reason that so many do now what the king, not insincerely, did then — for he ". . . took his ring from his hand, and gave it unto Haman the son of Hammedatha the Agagite, the Jews' enemy" (3:10).

To understand the interesting significance of this act, we need to turn to a parallel passage in the Old Testament found in the Book of Genesis. It concerns Pharaoh's relationship to Joseph, as expressed in what Pharaoh had to say to Joseph in the day that he took his ring from off his own hand and placed it upon Joseph's finger.

"Thou shalt be over my house, and according unto thy word shall all my people be ruled: only in the throne will I be greater than thou.

"And Pharaoh said unto Joseph, See, I have set thee over all the land of Egypt. And Pharaoh took off his ring from his hand, and put it upon Joseph's hand, and arrayed him in vestures of fine linen, and put a gold chain about his neck;

"And he made him to ride in the second chariot which he had; and they cried before him, Bow the knee: and he made him ruler over all the land of Egypt.

"And Pharaoh said unto Joseph, I am Pharaoh, and without thee shall no man lift up his hand or foot in all the land of Egypt" (Genesis 41:40-44).

In others words, this means that although Pharaoh retained his titular sovereignty, all the executive powers of government were vested in Joseph, and the symbol whereby this transfer of authority was sealed was Pharaoh's ring upon Joseph's finger.

In the same way, King Ahasuerus expressed his utter confidence in Haman by placing his ring upon Haman's finger, thus investing him with all the executive powers of government throughout the length and the breadth of his kingdom. Thereafter no inhabitant of the land might lift up his hand or foot save at Haman's behest, and under his total jurisdiction.

King Ahasuerus was sold out to Haman utterly, as the soul of the unregenerate is sold out to the flesh, and his behavior subject to the demands of a rebel regime that denies to God His right to be God.

"Then were the king's scribes called on the thirteenth day of the first month, and there was written according to all that Haman had commanded unto the king's lieutenants, and to the governors that were over every province, and to the rulers of every people of every province according to the writing thereof, and to every people after their language; in the name of king Ahasuerus was it written, and sealed with the king's ring.

"And the letters were sent by posts into all the king's provinces, to destroy, to kill, and to cause to perish, all Jews, both young and old, little children and women, in one day, even upon the thirteenth day of the twelfth month, which is the month Adar, and to take the spoil of them for a prey" (3:12, 13).

Thus the murderous decree was published "according to all that Haman had commanded," but "in the name of king Ahasuerus was it written, and sealed with the king's ring." What a startlingly accurate picture this gives of the human soul, dominated by the flesh and becoming party, however unwittingly, to every carnal ambition that would silence the voice of God and resist the claims of His Holy Spirit.

It is amazing with what enthusiasm man is prepared to allow his humanity to be prostituted by the devil, and yet even though he may seek to justify himself, and be persuaded of the virtue of his actions, there is an intangible restlessness within, that leaves him baffled and perplexed, for:

"The posts went out, being hastened by the king's commandment, and the decree was given in Shushan the palace. And the king and Haman sat down to drink; but the city Shushan was perplexed" (3:15).

There were strange whisperings in the city of Shushan and little groups of people huddled together on the streets. As the king and Haman sat down to drink in this unholy alliance, somehow the people sensed that all was not well with the kingdom — the city Shushan was perplexed.

Are there those indefinable moments in *your* life — the inaudible whisperings of a restless soul — moments of perplexity when you sense that all is not well with *you?*

4

The Spirit of Adoption,
Sackcloth and Ashes

WITH THE APPROACH OF THE DAY SET FOR THE MASSACRE, the shadow of death hung heavily over all the Jews in the land. Nothing but a change of government within the palace would have seemed to offer any hope of escape from the impending disaster, yet nothing seemed less likely than such a change of government.

If Mordecai held the key to their deliverance, the major problem still remained to be resolved — how to get the wrong man out and the right man in. Of all the lessons that the Book of Esther has to teach us, perhaps the most important is this — that to get the wrong man out and the right man in, it is necessary first to get the right man in to get the wrong man out!

Let us turn our attention for a moment to Mordecai and discover what we may about him.

"Now in Shushan the palace there was a certain Jew, whose name was Mordecai . . . a Benjamite;
"Who had been carried away from Jerusalem with the captivity which had been carried away with Jeconiah king of Judah, whom Nebuchadnezzar the king of Babylon had carried away" (2:5, 6).

35

This Mordecai is not to be confused with the one mentioned in the Book of Ezra, chapter two, verse two, though he too had been carried away into captivity in Babylon. Although the one may not be mistaken for the other, it is interesting to note that both in a unique way represent the gracious work of God, the Holy Spirit.

It is recorded in the first chapter of the Book of Ezra that the Lord so stirred up the spirit of Cyrus, king of Persia, that he made a proclamation throughout all his kingdom and he put it into writing saying,

> "Thus saith Cyrus king of Persia, The Lord God of heaven hath given me all the kingdoms of the earth; and he hath charged me to build him an house at Jerusalem, which is in Judah.
>
> "Who is there among you of all his people? his God be with him, and let him go up to Jerusalem, which is in Judah, and build the house of the Lord God of Israel . . .
>
> "Then rose up the chief of the fathers of Judah and Benjamin, and the priests, and the Levites, with all them whose spirit God had raised, to go up to build the house of the Lord which is in Jerusalem" (Ezra 1:2, 3, 5).

Among those who went up out of the captivity and returned to Jerusalem was this other Mordecai. Together with the rest, it was to be his noble office to rebuild the temple and to cleanse it so that it might be filled again with the glory of God. This of course is the special work of the Holy Spirit in your life and mine, that our bodies as temples of the living God might be filled afresh with His glory and be cleansed for His use as instruments of righteousness.

Similarly the picture presented to us in the Book

of Esther is of Mordecai as representing the Holy Spirit, gaining access to the life of King Ahasuerus representing the human soul; so that his own gracious and benevolent influence might replace the evil and malicious influence of the flesh as represented by Haman, and that throughout the kingdom, representing the human body, it might become gloriously obvious to the rest of the world that something wonderful had happened within the palace, changing completely the character of the land.

> "Therefore if any man be in Christ, he is a new creature: old things are passed away; behold, all things are become new.
> "And all things are of God . . ." (II Corinthians 5:17, 18).

THE HOLY SPIRIT RECEIVED

I am sure you have been wondering where Esther herself, from whom the Book has gained its title, fits into the story, so let us consider for a moment the role she has to play.

Before Mordecai could come into the life of the king, he had first to come into the life of Esther, just as the Holy Spirit must first be restored to the human spirit before He can begin to take control within the human soul. Esther, the queen, will represent the human spirit, just as Ahasuerus, the king, represents the human soul. The two are wedded the one to the other though they must not be confused the one for the other.

It is fascinating to discover by what means Mordecai came into the life of Esther, that through her he might come into the life of the king.

"And he brought up Hadassah, that is, Esther, his uncle's daughter: for she had neither father nor mother, and the maid was fair and beautiful; whom Mordecai, when her father and mother were dead, took for his own daughter" (2:7).

Mordecai came into the life of Esther on the basis of adoption!

What a beautiful picture this is of the Holy Spirit. As it became Mordecai's responsibility to educate and care for Esther, disciplining her life, guiding her steps and quickening within her a solemn sense of responsibility and divine destiny, so it is now the office of the Holy Spirit in your life to accomplish these things in you, leading you into all truth.

"For as many as are led by the Spirit of God, they are the sons of God.

"For ye have not received the spirit of bondage again to fear: but ye have received the spirit of adoption, whereby we cry, Abba, Father" (Romans 8:14, 15).

"But when the proper time had fully come, God sent His Son, born of a woman, born subject to [the regulations of] the Law,

"To purchase the freedom of (to ransom, to redeem, to atone for) those who were subject to the Law, that we might be adopted *and* have sonship conferred upon us — be recognized as [God's] sons.

"And because you [really] are (His) sons, God has sent the (Holy) Spirit of His Son into our hearts, crying, Abba (Father)! Father!" (Galatians 4:4-6, *Amplified Bible*).

The Holy Spirit is the Spirit of adoption!

It is the coming of the Holy Spirit into the human

spirit which constitutes that spiritual new birth by which we may be born into the family of God and become His children, and it is the presence of the Holy Spirit within the human spirit which constitutes the seal God sets upon this new relationship.

In the relationship that existed between Mordecai and Esther, we have a beautiful picture of the relationship that exists between the Holy Spirit and those, who by faith, have received Him. At the same time it is necessary to remind you that the faith through which we receive the Holy Spirit is the very faith through which we claim redemption through the blood of Christ — nor may the one be obtained without the other.

> "Christ hath redeemed us from the curse of the law, being made a curse for us: for it is written, Cursed is every one that hangeth on a tree:
> "That the blessing of Abraham might come on the Gentiles through Jesus Christ; that we might receive the promise of the Spirit through faith" (Galatians 3:13, 14).

It is when through faith you have claimed redemption, the forgiveness of your sins, through the blood of Christ shed vicariously for you, that God is able to send His Holy Spirit into your human spirit, and it is then that you begin to experience what John describes when he says, "He that believeth on the Son of God hath the witness in himself" — it is the witness of God which is greater than the witness of men.

> "The Spirit itself beareth witness with our spirit, that we are the children of God" (Romans 8:16).

> "Not by works of righteousness which we have done, but according to his mercy he saved us, by

the washing of regeneration, and renewing of the
Holy Ghost;

"Which he shed on us abundantly through Jesus
Christ our Saviour" (Titus 3:5, 6).

"In whom we have redemption through his
blood, the forgiveness of sins, according to the
riches of his grace" (Ephesians 1:7).

"In whom ye also trusted, after that you heard
the word of truth, the gospel of your salvation: in
whom also after that ye believed, ye were sealed
with that holy Spirit of promise" (Ephesians 1:13).

Have you claimed forgiveness from God through
the death of Christ on your behalf? Do you know that
you have received the Holy Spirit, in whose Person the
Lord Jesus has come to live within you, and who bears
witness to your spirit that you have become a child of
God? If not, would you do this now, before you read
another page, and settle this issue forever? You will be
so glad if you do!

The Holy Spirit Grieved

In chapter three we saw the Holy Spirit resisted;
in chapter two, the Holy Spirit received; but in the
opening verses of the fourth chapter we have another
picture — it is of the Holy Spirit grieved.

The Spirit of adoption has become the Spirit of
sackcloth and ashes, for we read, "When Mordecai per-
ceived all that was done, Mordecai rent his clothes, and
put on sackcloth with ashes, and went out into the
midst of the city, and cried with a loud and a bitter cry"
(4:1).

Esther herself was exceedingly grieved and bewildered by the situation and did her best, without success, to comfort Mordecai; but he would not be comforted. "She sent raiment to clothe Mordecai, and to take away his sackcloth from him: but he received it not" (4:4).

The picture presented to us is crystal clear, for although Mordecai had come into the life of Esther, he had not yet gained access through the palace into the inner counsels of the king. There, Haman still wore the ring and dominated the scene. This is the carnal or fleshly Christian.

If you have received the Lord Jesus Christ as your Redeemer, then the Holy Spirit, as we have already seen, has come to take up residence within your human spirit, and you have been born again and God has set His seal upon you as His child. But if that old, Adamic nature, the flesh, still dominates your soul and monopolizes your personality by coloring your thinking, sparking your ambitions, capturing your affections and subtly persuading your will into submission to its claims upon you, then you, too, are a carnal Christian. You are what Paul describes as a "babe in Christ," and the Holy Spirit will be grieved; He will become the Spirit of sackcloth and ashes.

> "However, brethren, I could not talk to you as to spiritual [men], but as to nonspiritual (men of the flesh, in whom the carnal nature predominates), as to mere infants [in the new life] in Christ — unable to talk yet!
>
> "For you are still (unspiritual, having the nature) of the flesh — under the control of ordinary impulses. For as long as [there are] envying and

jealousy *and* wrangling and factions among you, are you not unspiritual *and* of the flesh, behaving yourselves after a human standard *and* like mere (unchanged) men?" (I Corinthians 3:1, 3, *Amplified Bible*).

If the Holy Spirit is grieved within you, then you will not comfort Him by a change of raiment, but only by a change of government. He will never be comforted until the ring is on *His* finger, and Haman on the gallows!

Esther did not understand her own case, because as yet she did not know the character of Haman. You may be sure that on such occasions as those upon which he may have encountered the queen, Haman was as suave as they come — dripping with charm — for the flesh is well-tutored in the art of being disarmingly winsome as well as being brutally sadistic, degrading and cruel.

It was not his circumstances that bothered Mordecai, but the situation in the palace, for as long as the ring remained upon the wrong finger, there could only be disaster in the land, and a change of raiment would not put *that* right.

I wonder if you have been bewildered at this point in your Christian experience. You know you are converted, but beneath the outward practice and profession of your faith you are conscious of the inner nagging of a troubled spirit. True inner peace eludes you and you sigh for release. Perhaps like many another you have said to yourself, "I need a new church home. I do not think I fit into this community, but given a different spiritual environment I am sure I would make good." Soon you are on the road again, for this is not the first time it has happened.

You will not make good! You will simply create as much trouble in the next church as you made in the last, for there is nothing wrong with your spiritual environment, but there *is* something desperately wrong with *you!*

Fail to get that right, and you will be a spiritual tramp all the days of your life!

Preacher, you may say to yourself, "I need a new pastorate! I cannot get through to these people. They are so hopelessly unresponsive and I am wasting my gifts." No, preacher, blame the pulpit not the pew, and examine your own heart before you inflict yourself upon another weary congregation.

Perhaps you are a student at Bible college or seminary, and you have said to yourself, "I know that my spiritual life is at a pretty low ebb and that I am defeated in many areas of temptation, but I have been too busy with my exams to nourish my personal relationship to Jesus Christ. After all, student days only come once in a lifetime. I must admit I am not as concerned as I used to be about the lost, but of course when I get to the mission field that will all be different."

It will not be different! You will be a dead loss there as you are a dead loss now, for a change of geographical location will no more put the matter right than a change of pastorate or spiritual environment, as long as Haman is still strutting around in the palace, and wearing the king's ring.

You may get on board ship and sail to some far distant land, but wearing a topee and a khaki shirt, carving your way through the jungle with a Bible tucked under your arm, will not make you into a spiritual giant! If the Spirit of adoption has become the Spirit of sackcloth and ashes, then you may have got the Right Man in, but you have not yet got the wrong man out!

The ring is still on the wrong finger — if that persists, the noose may soon be round the wrong neck — and somehow that has got to be put right. It will take more than a change of raiment to do that.

You need a new Prime Minister!

5

Smack Wrong and Candy Right

ESTHER, BEING UNSUCCESSFUL IN HER ATTEMPTS TO COMfort Mordecai by her own devices, decided that the only sensible thing to do would be to allow Mordecai to explain the situation to her for himself, and give her his instructions. To this end she called for Hatach, "one of the king's chamberlains, whom he had appointed to attend upon her, and gave him a commandment to Mordecai, to know what it was, and why it was" (4:5).

Mordecai responded immediately to her request, as the Holy Spirit responds at once to you and to me the moment we are prepared to set aside our own preconceived notions, and allow Him to speak to us as the One whose office it is to convict us of our sin, and to lead us into all truth.

> "And Mordecai told him of all that had happened unto him, and of the sum of the money that Haman had promised to pay to the king's treasuries for the Jews, to destroy them.
> "Also he gave him the copy of the writing of the decree that was given at Shushan to destroy them, to shew it unto Esther . . ." (4:7, 8).

Before Haman could be brought to the gallows, Mordecai knew that it would be necessary first to convince Esther the queen of the wickedness of this sinister character, and of the murderous intent that lay beneath his charming manner.

It is just at this point, too, that true spiritual conviction begins. It is an activity of the Holy Spirit within the human spirit, before its fullest impact is made upon the soul.

It is perhaps difficult to locate the seat of human conscience, but it is important for us to recognize the fact that in addition to the moral conscience, there is an animal conscience, and it is easy for us to mistake the one for the other.

THE CONSCIENCE OF CONVENIENCE

The conscience of convenience acts upon the basis of what is consequentially right or wrong, as opposed to what is morally right or wrong, and it is located within the soul.

It is the animal conscience.

Maybe you can remember the first time you had a puppy in the home — a sweet, fluffy little thing! You had not had the puppy in the home for long, however, before you discovered that it needed to develop a conscience about certain matters!

Can you imagine slipping out to do some shopping some morning, just before lunch, leaving a nice juicy piece of steak upon the kitchen table? Needless to say, in your absence the puppy begins to make a reconnaissance, and climbing onto the kitchen table by easy stages, eyes the piece of steak with obvious admiration.

Now just put yourself in the puppy's position. If you were a hungry puppy and found yourself within chewing distance of a piece of steak, quite frankly, what would you do? Of course, the answer is a foregone conclusion — you would wrap yourself around it!

That is exactly what the puppy does, and when you return some time later, you find the steak inside the dog! The sweet, fluffy little thing!

Perhaps the first time it happens, after your first flush of indignation, you tend to take a charitable view of the matter, and somewhat amusingly recount the story to your friends. Not indeed, that you exempt the puppy altogether from a timely smack and a deep voiced "*Bad* dog! *Bad* dog!"

Mind you, to be quite honest, the puppy remains baffled at the exercise, quietly thinking to itself, "What extraordinary people these human beings are! Whatever can be wrong about a hungry dog eating juicy steak?"

When on some future occasion, and for the second time the puppy consumes your lunch, somehow the sweet, fluffy little thing is neither quite so sweet nor quite so fluffy!

Do you thrash that dog! Slowly, but without any moral enlightenment, the puppy gets the point, and when on yet another occasion the dog is left exposed by your carelessness to similar temptation it restrains its appetite, and gazing at the tempting morsel, with saliva dribbling down its cheeks, it says to itself, "I really do not see why I should not eat it, but the last time I did so that woman really got mad at me! The first time was not so bad, but the second time it really hurt when she thrashed me. It doesn't make sense to me, but maybe I'd better wait till she gets back."

The dog now has a conscience about stealing. Not, of course, that it has any moral value whatever, but it has learned that in life there are certain things that are smack wrong, and therefore better to be avoided for the consequences they incur.

Smack wrong!

In the meantime you may be teaching the dog to beg, and the thoughts that it has about you in the process would probably be less than flattering — "I can't think of anything more stupid than expecting me to sit on my hind legs and stick my paws out in the air! I'm just not made that way — I'm not that shape!" However, when the dog discovers that every earnest attempt receives its due reward, it learns that there are not only things in life that are smack wrong, but there are things in life that are candy right. Not right because they are right, but simply right because they get reward.

Candy right!

You may be shocked at the suggestion, but this is the primary stage in the education of a baby. You do not moralize in flowery language when it grabs the tablecloth and pulls the best china onto the floor. You teach it the hard way that this is one of the things in life which is smack wrong, and when it has swallowed the last mouthful of spinach and gets a piece of chocolate, it knows that this is one of the things in life which is candy right!

If you still fail to grasp what I am getting at, then ask yourself next time you are driving too fast in a speed restricted area, why it is you look so often and so anxiously in the mirror! It is probably because you are less *morally* concerned about the speed limit than you are *consequentially* concerned about the speed cop. It is smack wrong!

On this basis a thing may be socially right or socially wrong, ecclesiastically right or ecclesiastically wrong, financially right or financially wrong — or for that matter, evangelically right or evangelically wrong — without any real moral issue being involved on the part of the individual. He is simply trimming his behavior, on the one hand to avoid the smack, and on the other hand to get the candy.

I am convinced that there are tens of thousands of young people who profess to be Christians, but whose conduct within the evangelical context conforms to certain prescribed patterns that make them acceptable within the society to which they adhere, not because they have any deep spiritual conviction in the matter, but simply because they have been *evangelically* house-trained!

Send them off to a secular university, draft them into the armed forces, or in some other way detach them from the evangelical mould to which they have been conformed and the results are inevitably disastrous, because, confronted with the cold facts of life in a world of other standards, they discover that they never had any real conscience about anything — they simply did what their counselor told them to do.

THE CONSCIENCE OF CONVICTION

If the conscience of convenience determines only what is consequentially right and what is consequentially wrong, then the conscience of conviction determines what is morally right and what is morally wrong. In other words, what is right because it is right, and what is wrong because it is wrong — and for no other reason.

The conscience of convenience is *comparative* and will be subject to every changing wind of fashion, and will readily subscribe to the "new morality" which makes *immorality* acceptable to society. On the other hand, the conscience of conviction is *absolute* — as absolute as God Himself.

It may well be that within the human spirit of the unregenerate soul there remains a vestigial image of the righteousness and glory of God, in whose image man was created. It may be this which gives to the unregenerate, and even to the most degenerate, that strange inner sense of right and wrong which is so much nobler than that which derives only from the smack-wrong, candy-right conscience of convenience. Even so, it is unreliable. It may be seared, distorted, colored and twisted, by tradition, culture and circumstance, and in itself does not speak with that final authority that makes it impossible for a man to rationalize in such a way that wrong becomes right and right becomes wrong.

The first thing that the Holy Spirit does when He comes to take up residence within the spirit of a man, is to establish again those absolute standards of righteousness within the moral conscience, which reflect the very nature and character of God Himself.

This takes place even though such restored standards do not at once become articulate, as it were, within the soul. The regenerate sinner himself is not at first able to define this new principle of life, and all that he can say when challenged as to why he no longer does the things he did, or say the things he said, is this — "I do not know, I cannot explain it, but somehow deep down inside me I know now that to do and say these things is wrong."

This is why the deepest work of repentance within a man's life is brought about by the Holy Spirit subsequent to conversion, rather than prior to, or at conversion. It is true, of course, that there can be no genuine faith in Christ without some measure of repentance, but such initial repentance tends to stem more from the fear of the consequences of sin than from sorrow for the sinfulness of sin.

When the Holy Spirit begins to reveal to your human spirit the naked wickedness of the flesh, as Mordecai revealed to Esther the naked wickedness of Haman, such distressing conviction may result that you begin to wonder whether you were ever really saved. This is a healthy symptom, and one of the surest evidences of genuine spiritual new birth.

The Holy Spirit is like a man with a lamp entering a dark and dirty room, and what you have learned to live with in the dark becomes repugnant in the light.

In this way you come to realize the nature of your case and that you need a deeper work of grace than simply that which gets you out of hell and into heaven. You will begin to cry out with the psalmist of old, out of the bitterness of self discovery:

"Behold, I was shapen in iniquity; and in sin did my mother conceive me.

"Behold, thou desirest truth in the inward parts:

"Hide thy face from my sins, and blot out all mine iniquities.

"Create in me a clean heart, O God; and renew a right spirit within me. Cast me not away from thy presence; and take not thy holy Spirit from me" (Psalm 51:5, 6, 9-11).

Esther had to discover the kind of company she had been keeping in the palace — and it wasn't a pleasant discovery!

It is always an ugly experience when the Holy Spirit first introduces you to your own Haman, and rips the mask off his evil face.

You feel you want to flee with Peter — and weep bitterly (Luke 23:62)!

6

If I Perish, I Perish

SHOCKED, AND NOT A LITTLE FRIGHTENED TO DISCOVER that the affairs of the kingdom had been placed in such wicked hands, Esther was no less alarmed at Mordecai's explicit instructions, now that the enemy had been exposed.

Hatach had been sent by Mordecai, not only to show to Esther the copy of the writing of the decree that was given at Shushan to destroy the Jews, but also "to charge her that she should go in unto the king, to make supplication unto him, and to make request before him for her people" (4:8).

The queen knew full well, however, that to enter unsummoned into the presence of the king was to pass sentence of death upon herself, for such was the law of the land. It was not simply that those who crossed the threshold into the royal presence, without being called, would be put on trial and judged — sentence was automatic!

The moment Esther's foot crossed the forbidden line she knew that she would be as good as dead, save in the unlikely event that the king should hold out to her the golden scepter.

It was little wonder then that Mordecai's instructions came as a shock to the queen, and that her natural reaction was to recoil and protest.

Thus it was that she sent her reply:

"Again Esther spake unto Hatach, and gave him commandment unto Mordecai;

"All the king's servants, and the people of the king's provinces, do know, that whosoever, whether man or woman, shall come unto the king into the inner court, who is not called, there is one law of his to put him to death, except such to whom the king shall hold out the golden sceptre, that he may live: but I have not been called to come in unto the king these thirty days" (4:10, 11).

A fierce conflict now raged within the heart of Esther as she argued within herself. From chapter 2 verse 20 we understand that "Esther had not yet shewed her kindred nor her people; as Mordecai had charged her," but now she was to come out into the open and identify herself with God's people, God's purpose and God's power, and in doing so she would at once expose herself to Haman's hatred of the Jews.

Under these circumstances it seemed to be altogether unreasonable to sentence herself to death by seeking, so recklessly, an audience with the king. *"If Haman is as wicked and cunning as Mordecai makes him out to be, then at all costs I must survive, for I am indispensable to my people. Maybe I can outwit him; beat him at his own game and thwart his ugly plans — or maybe there's a better side to his character that needs to be encouraged. Perhaps, after all, there is some good in him that Mordecai has overlooked. But to die — self-*

*sentenced! No! There must be some more reasonable
alternative to death."*

Resisted, received and grieved — the picture now
is of the Holy Spirit quenched; for until Esther was prepared to die to her own ability to bring Haman to the
place of death, Mordecai would be unable to put him
on the gallows.

The lesson to be learned was as hard for Esther
then as it is for us today. It was not to be her responsibility to hang Haman, for that belonged to Mordecai.
It was to be her responsibility to do as she was told —
simply to obey instructions — even though death itself
might seem to be the only possible consequence.

As Esther had to die to her own ability to hang
Haman, so you, too, must die to your own ability to
deal with the flesh, for you cannot crucify yourself.
That is God's business. To walk in the Spirit is to have
such utter confidence in Him that you first seek His
instructions, then ask no further questions, but just do
as you are told. To all such the promise of God is that
they will not walk in the lusts of the flesh. The Holy
Spirit is fully able to deal with the flesh, and to put it
and to keep it in the place of death. It is His business
to hang Haman!

"And they told to Mordecai Esther's words.

"Then Mordecai commanded to answer Esther,
Think not with thyself that thou shalt escape in the
king's house, more than all the Jews.

"For if thou altogether holdest thy peace at this
time, then shall there enlargement and deliverance
arise to the Jews from another place; but thou and
thy father's house shall be destroyed: and who

knoweth whether thou art come to the kingdom for such a time as this?" (4:12-14).

Mordecai made it abundantly clear to Esther that she was not indispensable to God, but that God was essentially indispensable to her. He made it equally clear to her that a moment had come in her life which would be fraught with tremendous consequences — it would be decisive one way or the other.

Mordecai said to Esther in so many words, "You stand upon the threshold of that destiny for which you have been chosen and prepared, and if you choose right, then this can be your greatest hour. On the other hand, if you choose wrong — throw it all back into God's face and hold your peace to save your own skin — then do not flatter yourself that you will escape the consequences, for in seeking to preserve your own life you will lose it. If you are prepared to lose your life for God's sake, you will find it. This is your hour of destiny; choose wisely, do not throw it all away!"

I believe that such a moment comes in the life of every child of God — the moment when God's purpose for your life hangs delicately in the balance. It may be that at this very moment, these words find you too poised upon the threshold of that for which Christ redeemed you, and for which His Presence is waiting to empower you, and at one and the same time you are both frightened and excited at the prospect.

Fulfillment comes with the realization that you do not have in yourself what it takes. Death to all that you are in your own inadequacy is the only gateway through which you may enter into the fullness of all that Christ is, so that you may live miraculously in the power of

His resurrection, crying from the heart, "Lord Jesus,
I can't but You can, and that is all I need to know —
let's go!"

> "Then said Jesus unto his disciples, If any man
> will come after me, let him deny himself, and take
> up his cross, and follow me.
> "For whosoever will save his life shall lose it: and
> whosoever will lose his life for my sake shall find it"
> (Matthew 16:24, 25).

THE HOLY SPIRIT OBEYED

With the issues so clearly defined, the response
which Esther gave was both crisp and courageous, and
the picture that it presents of true discipleship is thrilling and dramatic.

> "Then Esther bade them return Mordecai this
> answer,
> "Go, gather together all the Jews that are present
> in Shushan, and fast ye for me, and neither eat nor
> drink three days, night or day: I also and my
> maidens will fast likewise; and so will I go in unto
> the king, which is not according to the law: and
> if I perish, I perish" (4:15, 16).

Esther the queen did not give away her beautiful
dresses, nor renounce the luxury of the royal court; she
neither relinquished her crown, nor dismissed her servants — she did not need to. The die was cast and the
decision had been made. The issue she had faced was
final and embraced all lesser issues. Esther now was
alive to God alone and dead to self and all self-interest.

Three days and three nights Esther was already
buried. Resolved to die, she had forsaken all — as good
as dead. As well she knew, only the golden scepter

could raise her from the dead on that third morning as she entered uninvited into the presence of the king.

What a wealth of significance there is to be found in this amazing picture. Three days and three nights! The third morning! Does this remind you of anything?

It was on the third morning that Joshua, taking his people into the place of death in the depths of Jordan, was preserved miraculously with the whole of Israel, by God's divine intervention, and brought through on dry ground into the Land of Promise. The people were raised from the dead on that third morning, to enter into all the good of that for which they had been redeemed out of Egypt.

Three days and three nights Jonah was in the belly of the whale, thrown overboard at his own request, dying to his own self-will and disobedience, buried with the weeds of his own waywardness wrapped about his head, only to be raised again, alive from the dead on the third morning; brought up on the seashore to be recommissioned for the task and to save a people from perishing.

It was on the third morning that "Abraham lifted up his eyes, and saw the place afar off" (Genesis 22:4). The place where a knife was to be plunged into the heart of Isaac, his only son; Isaac in whom was comprehended for Abraham all the promises of God, all his noblest aspiration — life itself, and as the knife flashed in the sunlight on that third morning, God provided the ram in the thicket as a substitute and raised Isaac "in a figure" from the dead (Hebrews 11:18, 19).

Willingness to die is the price that you must pay if you want to be raised from the dead and live and work and walk in the power of the third morning, sharing the resurrection life of Jesus Christ on earth. In this you are identified with Him in the relentless unfolding of God's redemptive purposes, which are to find their final consummation in the glorious appearing of our triumphant, risen Lord.

> "If ye then be risen with Christ, seek those things which are above, where Christ sitteth on the right hand of God.
> "Set your affections on things above, not on things on the earth.
> "For ye are dead, and your life is hid with Christ in God.
> "When Christ, who is our life, shall appear, then shall ye also appear with him in glory" (Colossians 3:1-4).

Lips quivering, every limb trembling, and with a heart thumping fit to burst, it was a pale-faced slip of a girl who stepped out on that third morning as she crossed the threshold of the royal court into the presence of the king, uninvited. She had nothing to lose, for she was already dead — self-sentenced; but she had everything to gain!

Compelled as though by some unseen, inner thrust, Esther threw her life away. Others gasped as they saw her go, for to them it was an act of reckless folly. But in her heart a little voice kept saying, "If I perish, I perish! If I perish, I perish! If I perish, I perish! God take the consequences!" And He did.

> "Now it came to pass on the third day, that Esther put on her royal apparel, and stood in the inner court of the king's house . . . and the king sat upon his royal throne in the royal house . . .

"And it was so, when the king saw Esther the
queen standing in the court, that she obtained fa-
vour in his sight: and the king held out to Esther
the golden sceptre that was in his hand. So Esther
drew near, and touched the top of the sceptre" (5:
1, 2).

God had raised her from the dead!

Dead to herself and alive to God, all responsibility
now rested fairly and squarely upon the shoulders of
Mordecai. Esther knew the emancipation of obedience.
There were no more issues for her to face — only instructions to obey.

7

The Gallows in the Garden

DEAD MEN CANNOT DIE, NOR CAN THEY BE FRIGHTENED, and responsibility does not rest too heavily upon their shoulders! In fact, there is nothing quite so relaxing as being dead — dead, I mean, to your own ability to hang Haman! Dead in point of fact, to your own ability to accomplish anything, Haman or no Haman, apart from Jesus Christ.

Of course, you can afford to die, once you have become utterly convinced that death to yourself is to trade what you are for what Christ is — but it is right at this point that unbelief rears its ugly head. If you are not wholly convinced that Jesus Christ is willing and able to take over, then you will hang on to what you are like grim death. You may be absolutely certain that you will never know that deep-seated peace that comes from allowing the Lord Jesus Christ to assume responsibility and to get into business.

There is a pragmatic state of mind in some to which this total repudiation of self-effort is abhorrent, resulting sometimes in hostility — a hostility borne of self-justification. It is necessary to be patient with such people because they are often very dedicated in their desire to serve God; but the whole concept of a Christian life which is nothing more nor less than Jesus Christ Himself in action, baffles them as thoroughly as the confidence and peace it gives eludes them.

This in itself would be surprising, were it not for the fact that no spiritual truth can dawn save by revelation. The principle involved was perfectly enunciated by the Lord Jesus Christ Himself, who for thirty-three years allowed the Father to be in Him then, through the Holy Spirit, what He Himself wants to be in us now, through the Holy Spirit. He "never answered back when insulted; when He suffered He did not threaten to get even; He left His case in the Hands of God Who always judges fairly" (I Peter 2:23, *Living Letters*).

The Lord Jesus reckoned with the Father and acted at all times on the assumption that His Father was handling the situation, only always taking care to obey instructions. He learned obedience, obedience unto death; and now as God, He does not ask you or me to be any weaker or any more foolish than He was prepared to be Himself; for the cross was both the weakness of God and the foolishness of God.

> "For though he was crucified through weakness, yet he liveth by the power of God. . . .
> "Because the foolishness of God is wiser than men; and the weakness of God is stronger than men" (II Corinthians 13:4; I Corinthians 1:25).

This is what baffled the disciples. They thought that the Lord Jesus Christ was hopelessly passive, and that He was failing to come to grips with reality; He seemed bent on drifting to disaster. Why did He not get organized? Why did He not cash in on His popularity with the crowd, or pull some political strings? After all, money speaks, and surely the rich young ruler could have exercised a positive influence in getting the movement off the ground!

Whenever the Lord Jesus Christ performed some notable miracle and someone was healed, why did He avoid those very obvious opportunities for wide publicity and tell everyone to keep their mouths shut? Why did He not throw His weight around, project His personality, exercise His authority and confound His foes once and for all by an overwhelming, crushing, vindication of His deity? Why did He not let folk know just who He was and where He had come from? Why did He not justify His claim to equality with the Father and wipe the floor with His enemies? Why this pitiable show of weakness and this apparent foolishness? Did He not have what it took to be smart? These are some of the questions which must have crowded in upon the minds of His disciples. They did not want the cross, but then of course they did not believe in the Resurrection!

The Lord Jesus Christ could afford to be reviled; He could afford to be spat on; He could afford to be weak and He could afford to be foolish in the eyes of silly, sinful men, because He knew the One by whom He had been sent and the One into whose hands He had committed His Spirit — not only in death, but in thirty-three years of life. He could afford to do as He was told, and He could afford to die, because He knew that Someone else was taking care of the consequences.

If you are not yet prepared to do as you āre told, no matter how weak it may make you look, or foolish it may seem to other people, then whatever you may believe about the Resurrection of the Lord Jesus Christ, it is still purely academic — you have not yet entered into the good of it. The life of Jesus Christ within you makes human circumstances irrelevant when it comes to the point of obedience to His clear instructions; for to share His life now as He once shared His Father's life on earth then, is to know as He did, that Someone else is taking care of the consequences.

I do not mean by this that God's purposes are always irrational in the light of human circumstance, nor that there is peculiar virtue in being eccentric or foolhardy. It is simply that you become delightfully detached from the pressure of circumstance, and it ceases to be the criterion in the decisions which you make. You do as you are told whether God's instructions appear to be compatible with the immediate situation or not, and you leave God to vindicate Himself and to justify the course of action upon which, at His command, you have embarked.

Upon this basis Abraham could afford to say to Lot, "Let there be no strife, I pray thee, between me and thee, between my herdmen and thy herdmen; for we be brethren. Is not the whole land before thee? Separate thyself, I pray thee, from me: if thou wilt take the left hand, then I will go to the right; or if thou depart to the right hand, then I will go to the left" (Genesis 13:8, 9). Here was restful indifference to what others might reasonably have argued was legitimate self-interest. Lot could take the left or Lot could take the right, or for that matter Lot could take the lot, but God's covenant was still with Abraham—and he knew it. That was all that Abraham really needed to know.

Moses could afford to defy Pharaoh and put his feet in the Red Sea, as Joshua could defy Jericho, and put his feet in Jordan, as long as they knew that God would take the consequences and give the Egyptians a ducking and the Canaanites a thrashing!

With the jawbone of an ass or Gideon's three hundred; with Aaron's rod or David's sling; with a pinch of salt or a little pot of oil, God insists on doing the impossible and vindicates the faith of those who will obey Him.

Perhaps you understand what Paul meant when he wrote in so many words — "I was in fact crushed, overwhelmed and desperate. I feared I would never live through it. I thought I was doomed to die and saw how powerless I was to help myself" (I Corinthians 2:8, *Living Letters*). But I wonder whether you have gone on as Paul did, to know God as the One who is overwhelmingly adequate, no matter how hopeless the situation may seem to be, for he continued, ". . . but that was good, for then I put everything into the hands of God, Who alone could save me, for He can even raise the dead, and He did . . ."

Only pass the sentence of death upon yourself and you can afford to do as you are told, even as Esther did, though no doubt she was somewhat mystified at the instructions which she received. She knew then that she did not have to ask questions.

Have you come to the place in your relationship
with the Lord Jesus Christ where you have stopped in-
terrogating Him about His intentions?

ESTHER THROWS A PARTY!

"Then said the king unto her, What wilt thou,
queen Esther? and what is thy request? it shall be
even given thee to the half of the kingdom.

"And Esther answered, If it seem good unto the
king, let the king and Haman come this day unto
the banquet that I have prepared for him.

"Then the king said, Cause Haman to make
haste, that he may do as Esther hath said. So the
king and Haman came to the banquet that Esther
had prepared" (5:3-5).

No doubt upon Mordecai's advice the tables were
spread, a sumptuous meal was prepared, and Esther
invited the king and Haman to dinner.

If Haman was to hang, this was certainly a most
unusual way to lead a man to the gallows. But Esther
did not question Mordecai's wisdom — she did as she
was told; and indeed when again the king gave her the
opportunity to lay before him her petition, the queen
replied, "My petition and my request is; If I have found
favor in the sight of the king, and if it please the king
to grant my petition, and to perform my request, let the
king and Haman come to the banquet that I shall prepare for them, and I will do tomorrow as the king hath
said" (5:7, 8).

As though to feed the man once were not enough,
Haman is invited with the king to a further banquet the
following day. If it is possible to kill a man with kindness, no doubt it must be possible to hang a man with

hospitality! Of one thing we may be sure — no matter how curious Esther may have been as to the ultimate course of events, Haman was already on his way out.

THE FLY IN THE OINTMENT

Needless to say, Haman was proud fit to burst at this double invitation to dine with the queen and "went forth that day joyful and with a glad heart" (5:9). When Haman got home he called for his friends and Zeresh, his wife, and gave them a typical exhibition of the flesh in boastful, loud-mouthed self-approval.

> "And Haman told them of the glory of his riches, and the multitude of his children, and all the things wherein the king had promoted him, and how he had advanced him above the princes and servants of the king. Haman said moreover, Yea, Esther the queen did let no man come in with the king unto the banquet that she had prepared but myself; and to morrow am I invited unto her also with the king" (5:11, 12).

With a show of nauseating conceit, Haman indicates that he is not only now the king's favorite, but the queen's favorite too — and to the exclusion of all others. It is characteristic of the flesh to seek its own aggrandizement at the expense of everyone else.

Reading between the lines, and in so many words, what Haman had to say to his friends was this, "Apart from the king, the queen would not let anyone else come to the banquet but myself, and confidentially, between you, me and the gatepost, I do not think she was really enthusiastic about the king being there either!" The flesh has an unlimited capacity for self-deception when it comes to enhancing its own reputation.

Basking as he was, however, in his own limelight, there was just one thing that spoiled it all. It was the one big fly in the ointment, for ". . . when Haman saw Mordecai in the king's gate, that he stood not up, nor moved for him, he was full of indignation against Mordecai" (5:9). There was one person who still remained unbowed in his presence, and who was patently unimpressed, and in a sudden fit of fury Haman protested to his wife and friends, "Yet all this availeth me nothing, so long as I see Mordecai the Jew sitting at the king's gate" (5:13).

The Holy Spirit always exposes the flesh for what it is and there is nothing more infuriating to the carnally-minded Christian, than when the spiritually discerning remain wholly unimpressed in spite of so much self-advertisement.

You have probably heard of the man who boasted to his friend, "I am a self-made man!" and his friend replied drily, and not a little unkindly, "That just demonstrates the horrors of unskilled labor!"

> "Then said Zeresh his wife and all his friends unto him, Let a gallows be made of fifty cubits high, and to morrow speak thou unto the king that Mordecai may be hanged thereon: then go thou in merrily with the king unto the banquet. And the thing pleased Haman; and he caused the gallows to be made" (5:14).

"If you are as popular with the king and with the queen as you say you are," suggested Haman's friends, "then build a gallows in your garden and speak to the king tomorrow before the second banquet takes place, that Mordecai may be hanged thereon. Then you will have nothing further to disturb your peace of mind or thwart your ambitions." Haman was highly delighted at the suggestion, and it was not long before the rope was swinging in the breeze.

All this was to take place between the two banquets, before ever Esther would have a further audience with the king, and on the face of it things were not looking too rosy for Mordecai. Had Esther known what was going on behind the scenes, she might well have been tempted to wonder whether all was really going according to plan.

In the little time that still remained, the all-important issue would have to be decided — for there was a gallows in the garden. Who was going to hang? Haman or Mordecai? Ultimately, this is the all-important issue that must be decided in *your* heart, as it must be decided within the heart of every true believer.

If Christ is on the cross, then self is on the throne; but if self is on the cross, then Christ is on the throne.

There is a gallows in the garden!

Who is going to swing?

8

Doom of Duplicity —
Haman Begins to Fall!

LOBSTER!

Mind you, it does not exactly say lobster — it could have been gorganzola cheese. Something rich too late at night, perhaps: but whatever it may have been, "on that night could not the king sleep" (6:1).

That night, of all nights — the night between the two banquets, just when Mordecai seemed to have been in such mortal danger, and on the eve of his intended execution—precisely that night the king could not sleep. He tossed and he turned, he threw the blankets off and he pulled the blankets on, he lay on his back, he lay on his side, he counted sheep and recited the alphabet—but still he could not sleep. At last, in desperation, he called for the book of records and "they were read before the king."

God's timings are always perfect. Not till all seemed lost and the knife was flashing in the sun did God tell Abraham to throw the knife away. Though due to die at dawn, Peter was delivered from his chains and from the prison by the angel of the Lord, who thus cheated Herod of his prey. Not by chance did Philip meet the eunuch in the desert, nor Paul encounter Lydia by the riverside — these were those divine providences by which God accomplishes His divine ends. "I being in the way," said Abraham's servant, "the Lord led me," and he brought Rebecca home to Isaac.

As the pages of the book were read upon this restless night, "it was found written, that Mordecai had told of Bigthan and Teresh, two of the king's chamberlains, the keepers of the door, who sought to lay hand on the king Ahasuerus" (6:2). The king suddenly became aware that Mordecai had been the means of his deliverance from those who had plotted his destruction.

The story is tucked away in the last three verses of the second chapter.

> "In those days, while Mordecai sat in the king's gate, two of the king's chamberlains, Bigthan and Teresh, of those which kept the door, were wroth, and sought to lay hand on the king Ahasuerus.
>
> "And the thing was known to Mordecai, who told it unto Esther the queen; and Esther certified the king thereof in Mordecai's name.
>
> "And when inquisition was made of the matter, it was found out; therefore they were both hanged on a tree; and it was written in the book of the chronicles before the king."

It was not that the king was unfamiliar with the facts, for he had been instructed long since in the story of his deliverance, but never before had it come to him with such startling significance as upon this troubled, sleepless night. Somehow he had never paused to think that but for Mordecai's intervention he would have fallen prey to the assassin's knife — dead and buried.

In a cold sweat and startled at the thought of it, the king cried, "What honour and dignity hath been done to Mordecai for this? Then said the king's servants that ministered unto him, There is nothing done for him." His servants might well have added, "You never seemed to care and it did not appear to be of any real concern to you. You were preoccupied with other things, and this man has gone completely unrewarded."

It is possible for a man to live for many years strangely unmoved by the amazing love of God in Christ, and though professing saving faith, so to be preoccupied with other things, that the momentous fact of redemption through the precious blood of Jesus remains a matter of secondary importance.

The facts are known but unrelated, until that moment of fuller revelation, when almost inexplicably, the significance of the cross stands out vividly in bold relief, and a troubled, restless soul is suddenly confronted with the claims of a neglected Saviour. At the sight of the wounds in His hands and in His feet the heart cries out to God, "What honor and dignity hath been done to Him for this?"

The answer to this question today may be as crushing to us as that given then to the king was to him — "There is nothing done for him." Filled with remorse and a quickened sense of urgency in the matter the king said, "Who is in the court?" Something had to be done and done at once to right this wrong, and the king sought someone to whom he might entrust this solemn responsibility.

Who do you think was there? The picture is magnificent! Who do you think came into the court just at that psychological moment?

> "Now Haman was come into the outward court of the king's house, to speak unto the king to hang Mordecai on the gallows that he had prepared for him. And the king's servants said unto him, Behold, Haman standeth in the court. And the king said, Let him come in" (6:5).

Just as the king was preparing to honor Mordecai, Haman came in for permission to hang him!

Remember however, what we have already learned in the previous chapter. Though the Holy Spirit may bring conviction within the human spirit, it does not necessarily become articulate at once, nor discernible within the soul. The king, as a picture of the human soul, had not yet become aware of the wickedness of Haman as it had already been revealed so convincingly by Mordecai to Esther. Indeed, the king was still fully persuaded of this man's integrity, and to whom could he more confidently entrust the responsibility of honoring Mordecai than to Haman himself? "So Haman came in. And the king said unto him, What shall be done unto the man whom the king delighteth to honour? Now Haman thought in his heart, To whom would the king delight to do honour more than to myself?" (6:6).

Utterly ego-centric and completely obsessed with his own self-importance, it seemed inconceivable to Haman that the king would wish to honor anyone but himself, and unable to think save in terms of self-aggrandizement, all the measures he suggested were designed for his own advantage.

"And Haman answered the king, For the man whom the king delighteth to honour,

"Let the royal apparel be brought which the king useth to wear, and the horse that the king rideth upon, and the crown royal which is set upon his head:

"And let this apparel and horse be delivered to the hand of one of the king's most noble princes, that they may array the man withal whom the king delighteth to honour, and bring him on horseback through the street of the city, and proclaim before him, Thus shall it be done to the man whom the king delighteth to honour" (6:7-9).

Haman could just fancy himself being led through the streets of the city proudly acknowledging the thunderous applause of the excited crowds, gorgeously arrayed in the king's apparel and with the crown royal set upon his head. After all, what could be more logical than this; he was the king's favorite, wasn't he? And the queen's blue-eyed boy? Enjoying as he did such overwhelming approval, the little matter of putting Mordecai on the gallows in the garden was quite obviously a foregone conclusion.

Haman could think of nothing more delicious than to see his archenemy swinging by the neck as the glorious "grande finale" to a day of royal acclamation.

"Then the king said to Haman, Make haste, and take the apparel and the horse, as thou hast said, and do even so to Mordecai the Jew, that sitteth at the king's gate: let nothing fail of all that thou hast spoken" (6:10).

I would love to have seen Haman's face, wouldn't you? Livid with rage and white as a sheet, with the

last drop of blood drained from his features, Haman
was careful to control his feelings. He did not explode;
he was far too clever for that. Something quite obviously
had happened to the king, and although he did not know
that the king had rediscovered Mordecai through the
reading of the book, he somehow knew that to defy him
in his present state of mind would be more than his
life was worth.

It is dangerous for the flesh when you rediscover
Christ through the reading of the Book!

It was now for Haman a question of self-preserva-
tion, and he was prepared even to go through the motions of honoring Mordecai if this was the price of survival.

The king was not insincere in enlisting the services
of Haman in his desire to honor Mordecai; he was
simply ignorant of the character of the man. For the
same reason you too may well have harnessed the
energy of the flesh in an otherwise quite genuine desire
to honor the Lord Jesus in your life. What you will discover now is what the king discovered then, that the
flesh, which has its origin in Satan, will go along with
you. It is quite prepared to engage in every form of
Christian activity, even though this may seem to honor
Christ, if that be the only chance of survival.

The flesh will sing in the church choir, superintend
the Sunday school, preside at a meeting of the deacons,
preach from the pulpit, organize an evangelistic cru-
sade, go to Bible School and volunteer for the mission
field, and a thousand and one things more (all of which
may in themselves be otherwise legitimate), if only it
can keep its neck out of the noose.

It is characteristic of the spiritually immature that they are unable to discern between good and evil (Hebrews 5:13, 14) and the baby Christian, like the foolish Galatians, "having begun in the Spirit" still tries to be "made perfect by the flesh" (Galatians 3:3).

> "Then took Haman the apparel and the horse, and arrayed Mordecai, and brought him on horseback through the street of the city, and proclaimed before him, Thus shall it be done unto the man whom the king delighteth to honour" (6:11).

So Haman did what he was commanded, and seemingly to the king's entire satisfaction, for he was so enthusiastic in his desire to honor Mordecai that he was altogether unsuspecting of Haman's duplicity.

We must be particularly patient with those whose lack of understanding allows a genuine love for the Lord Jesus to be satisfied with, and sometimes to be quite enthusiastic about Christian activities involving means and methods which, to the more discerning, are heavily contaminated by the flesh. These are more deserving of instruction than rebuke — for they are still in their spiritual babyhood.

Mordecai returned again to the king's gate, but "Haman hasted to his house mourning and having his head covered" (6:12). To Zeresh, his wife, and to all his friends, Haman lodged his complaint and poured out the sorry story of his bitter humiliation, and their response to his lament could hardly be described as particularly comforting. "You are thrashed!" they said. "You are beaten!" The flesh has few friends in its adversity and little to comfort it in the day of its calamity. "If Mordecai be of the seed of the Jews, before whom thou hast begun to fall, thou shalt not prevail against him, but shalt surely fall before him. And while they were yet talking with him, came the king's chamberlains, and hasted to bring Haman unto the banquet that Esther had prepared" (6:13; 14).

With their discomforting prophecies of impending disaster still upon the lips of Haman's friends, the king's chamberlains burst in upon this gloomy scene, and hasted to bring him to the banquet that Esther had prepared.

Time had run out on Haman! The table was laid and the stage was set. From a gallows in his garden, fifty cubits high, a rope swung gently in the breeze, and in the heart of Haman there was a sense of doom.

The doom of duplicity!

9

The Moment of Truth

THE FLESH WILL THREATEN, SHOUT, STRUT, DOMINEER, sulk, plot, creep, beg, plead or sob — whatever the situation may demand in the interests of its own survival. In the wicked heart of Haman there were terrible forebodings as he went with the king to the banquet, for he knew that he was beaten. If the king had come to know the truth about Mordecai, it would not be long before he came to know the truth about Haman himself.

The flesh hates to be exposed for what it is and will fight desperately to avoid that awful moment of truth — that moment when the Holy Spirit rips the mask from its sickly face.

No doubt Haman planned to be on his best behavior at this second banquet, and he would try to be unusually convincing; though maybe few of the servants failed to notice his unusual nervousness.

When the Holy Spirit begins to convict you, bearing witness to your human spirit that the Lord Jesus Christ is being denied His rightful place in your life, the old Adam-nature within you becomes irritable and edgy. Yet at one and the same time it will seek to produce the most plausible arguments in justification of its own illegitimate activities.

Something told Haman that he could expect no mercy at the hands of Mordecai once Mordecai had gained the ear and confidence of the king, and the flesh knows that it cannot bluff its way out of a direct encounter with the Holy Spirit. It can only echo the words of Ahab to Elijah — "Hast thou found me, oh mine enemy?" And the Holy Spirit replies as He did through Elijah then — "I have found thee: because thou hast sold thyself to work evil in the sight of the LORD" (I Kings 21:20).

> "And the king said again unto Esther on the second day at the banquet of wine, What is thy petition, queen Esther? and it shall be granted thee: and what is thy request? and it shall be performed, even to the half of the kingdom" (7:2).

This must have been a tremendous moment for Esther, for until now, though acting in obedience to Mordecai, her total commitment had not brought her into direct conflict with Haman. She had shared the palace with him, living within the same four walls and beneath the same roof, and exchanging courtesies, but from now on there was to be no more compromise. Haman had to be named — exposed to the king as he had already been exposed to her. Judgment pronounced by Mordecai had to be echoed now in the presence of the king and in the very face of the enemy. From this moment there could be no going back, for this was the point of no return.

Haman held his breath and his brow broke out in beads of icy perspiration as Esther answered the king —

"If I have found favor in your sight, O King, and if it please the king, let my life be given me at my petition, and my people at my request; For we are sold, I and my people, to be destroyed, slain, and wiped out of existence! But if we had been sold for bondmen and bondwomen, I would have held my tongue, for our affliction is not to be compared with the damage this will do to the king" (7:3, 4, *Amplified Bible*).

Not only had the king become kindly disposed toward Mordecai, but Haman now discovered that the queen herself was wholly identified with his archenemy, and with that people whose God-given laws were in such direct conflict with those that had their origin in himself. Within a matter of minutes now the king would come to realize that the assassin's knife was pointed at the heart of the palace, and that Esther whom he loved would fall prey to this commandment published at Haman's behest — "To destroy, to kill, and to cause to perish, all Jews, both young and old, little children and women, in one day" (3:13).

Haman had persuaded the king that such a commandment would be in his own best interests, whereas it was designed only to satisfy Haman's wicked pride. He would then be able to silence the voice of Mordecai, and remove any threat to his own ability to usurp and abuse the authority of the king. He could exploit the kingdom to his own wicked ends.

"Then the king Ahasuerus answered and said unto Esther the queen, Who is he, and where is he, that durst presume in his heart to do so?

"And Esther said, The adversary and enemy is

this wicked Haman. Then Haman was afraid before the king and the queen.

"And the king arising from the banquet of wine in his wrath went into the palace garden: and Haman stood up to make request for his life to Esther the queen; for he saw that there was evil determined against him by the king" (7:5-7).

The enemy had been unmasked, and for the king the issues were now clear — he had to choose between Haman and Esther. This was the moment of truth — as it is for every human soul to whom has come the revelation of the Holy Spirit, through the human spirit, of the wickedness of sin.

It is so easy to become familiar with Bible language without receiving any real revelation of truth. God wants to bring you, no matter how bitter may be the experience, to the place of self-discovery. Thus it may dawn upon your soul in startling reality, in the words of Paul the apostle — "We know that the Law is spiritual; but I am a creature of the flesh (carnal, unspiritual), having been sold into slavery under [the control of] sin" (Romans 7:14, *Amplified Bible*).

This is what Romans 7 is all about. It describes the exploitation of the soul of man by the subtle principle of sin within, and there is no more lucid illustration of this than that which is to be found in the Book of Esther, in the part played by Haman in the life of the king.

"For I do not understand my own actions — I am baffled, bewildered. I do not practice *or* accomplish what I wish, but I do the very thing that I loathe [which my moral instinct condemns]. . . .

"However, it is no longer I who do the deed, but the sin [principle] which is at home in me *and* has possession of me. For I know that nothing good dwells within me, that is, in my flesh. . . .

"Now if I do what I do not desire to do, it is no longer I doing it — it is not myself that acts — but the sin [principle] which dwells within me [fixed and operating in my soul].

"So I find it to be a law [of my being] that when I want to do what is right *and* good, evil is ever present with me *and* I am subject to its insistent demands.

"For I endorse *and* delight in the Law of God in my inmost self — with my new nature.

"But I discern in my bodily members . . . a different law (rule of action) at war against the law of my mind (my reason) and making me a prisoner to the law of sin. . . .

"O unhappy *and* pitiable *and* wretched man that I am! Who will release *and* deliver me from [the shackles of] this body of death?

"O thank God! — He will! through Jesus Christ" (Romans 7:15, 17, 18, 20-25, *Amplified Bible*).

Here, clearly defined, is the conflict.

There is the inner witness of the Holy Spirit to your human spirit to all that is good and right and noble, and every act and attitude of sin is an offense to your moral conscience, thus enlightened. This part of you says — "I acknowledge *and* agree that the Law is good (morally excellent) *and* that I take sides with it. For I endorse *and* delight in the Law of God in my inmost self — with my new nature" (Romans 7:16, 22, *Amplified Bible*). It is this part of you which is represented by Esther.

There is then that other part of you represented by Haman, described by Paul as — "The sin [principle] which dwells within me [fixed and operating in my soul]" (Romans 7:20, *Amplified Bible*). The moment of truth will come for you when, together with Esther, you quit exchanging courtesies with the flesh and repudiate it to its face, naming it for the treacherous, wicked, worthless thing it is — without any salvageable content and fit only for the gallows!

At this climactic stage in your Christian life you realize that there can be no compromise with the flesh, and that peaceful coexistence with a principle satanically hostile to the law of God and to the re-establishment of His sovereignty within your soul, is now beyond the bounds of possibility.

You realize that it was never God's purpose to improve the flesh, to re-educate or tame it — let alone Christianize it. It has always been God's purpose that the flesh, condemned, sentenced and crucified with Jesus Christ, might be left buried in the tomb and replaced by the resurrection life of the Lord Jesus Christ Himself. He must wear the ring upon *His* finger, and once more exercise control in the area of your mind, your emotions and your will, expressing Himself through your personality.

Paul described this clearly in his concern for the Ephesian Christians, when he wrote —

"For this cause I bow my knees unto the Father of our Lord Jesus Christ . . .

"That he would grant you, according to the riches of his glory, to be strengthened with might by his Spirit in the inner man;

"That Christ may dwell in your hearts by faith
. . ." (Ephesians 3:14-17).

Here again the "inner man" is represented by
Esther as the human spirit, strengthened and encouraged by Mordecai as the Holy Spirit, and "your hearts"
are represented by King Ahasuerus, in his palace, as
the human soul.

> "And the king arising from the banquet of wine
> in his wrath went into the palace garden: and Ha-
> man stood up to make request for his life to Esther
> the queen; for he saw that there was evil deter-
> mined against him by the king.
>
> "Then the king returned out of the palace garden
> into the place of the banquet of wine; and Haman
> was fallen upon the bed whereon Esther was. Then
> said the king, Will he force the queen also before
> me in the house? As the word went out of the
> king's mouth, they covered Haman's face" (7:7, 8).

Haman recognized now how deeply the influence
of Mordecai had penetrated the palace, and the arro-
gance of this would-be murderer was turned into the
sulky, sentimental pleadings of a frightened coward.

Haman the Agagite was proving true to his breed,
as the flesh itself — to the spiritually discerning — must
always bear the stamp of its satanic pedigree. History
was simply repeating itself, for you will remember that
after King Saul had fallen prey to the suave persuasions
and deceptive charm of Agag, king of the Amalekites,
and God had rejected him because he had rejected the
word of the Lord, that Samuel moved into the situation. He announced against Agag the sentence of death
which God had passed upon him, and from which Saul
had spared him.

"Bring ye hither to me Agag the king of the Amalekites," Samuel cried. "And Agag came unto him delicately. And Agag said, Surely the bitterness of death is passed" (I Samuel 15:32). In his own persuasively deceptive way Agag the Amalekite tried to bluff his way through, as though it would be quite unfair of God to be as merciless to him as he had been to others. "And Samuel said, As thy sword hath made women childless, so shall thy mother be childless among women. And Samuel hewed Agag in pieces before the LORD in Gilgal" (I Samuel 15:33).

How quickly the boastful swagger of the flesh, in the day of its ascendancy, can be reduced to the sobbing cry of self-pity when the moment of truth has come. Beware of this subtilty, and never be sorry for yourself — just be sorry for your sin! If your pride is hurt and you feel that you have been misjudged, and you become all sensitive and begin to sulk, you can be quite certain that it is only Haman groveling in the dirt, sobbing for the mercy he doesn't deserve.

Haman is fit only for the gallows!

"And Harbonah, one of the chamberlains, said before the king, Behold also, the gallows fifty cubits high, which Haman had made for Mordecai, who had spoken good for the king, standeth in the house of Haman. Then the king said, Hang him thereon.

"So they hanged Haman on the gallows that he had prepared for Mordecai. Then was the king's wrath pacified" (7:9, 10).

What an amazing picture this is! Haman hanging

on his own gallows — the gallows that he had prepared for Mordecai.

Nineteen hundred years ago it was a Roman gallows, and of those who put Him there the Lord Jesus said — "Ye are of your father the devil, and the lusts of your father ye will do. He was a murderer from the beginning, and abode not in the truth, because there is no truth in him" (John 8:44). How Satan must have relished the idea of God's Son hanging on that cross! How carefully the plot was laid, as Satan entered into the heart of Judas Iscariot and persuaded him on that awful night to go out into the darkness and betray his Lord for thirty pieces of silver. With what ecstatic delight Satan must have incited the crowd as they looked and stared upon Him shouting — "He saved others; himself he cannot save" (Matthew 27:42). This was to be his hour of triumph — but one thing he did not know!

There was sterner business to be accomplished upon the cross than Satan ever guessed. This was not just the sentence of death upon a man by fellow men — a spectacular public execution, or the untimely end of a noble martyr, who drifted to disaster because He lived before His day and generation. Die indeed He did, as men must die, whose blood is spilt; it was not the Son, however, but Satan himself who bore the mortal blow of God's relentless wrath, as the Saviour tasted death for every man.

"Forasmuch then as the children are partakers of flesh and blood, he also himself likewise took part of the same; that through death he mighty destroy

him that had the power of death, that is, the devil"
(Hebrews 2:14).

"For what the law could not do, in that it was
weak through the flesh, God sending his own Son
in the likeness of sinful flesh, and for sin, condemned sin in the flesh" (Romans 8:3).

When the Lord Jesus Christ died for you, He not
only paid the price of your redemption, but identified
with Him there and nailed to His cross, was that old
sinful nature that for so long has dominated your soul
and frustrated all your hopes. This is something which
God wants you to know; for "We know that our old
(unrenewed) self was nailed to the cross with Him in
order that [our] body, [which is the instrument] of sin,
might be made ineffective *and* inactive for evil, that
we might no longer be the slaves of sin" (Romans 6:6,
Amplified Bible).

This is the truth being expressed in the language
of the Book of Esther, when Haman was hanged upon
the gallows that he had prepared for Mordecai. No
longer might Haman exercise the executive powers of
government and abuse the king's authority. No longer
would he bring disrepute upon the kingdom, through
his malicious evil influence over the behavior of this
people throughout the length and breadth of the land.
The kingdom, representing the human body, was no
longer to be the instrument of his evil acts, but by his
death it would become ineffective and inactive for evil.

As Haman hung by the neck, so the stage was set
for that radical change of government which would
produce so great a change in behavior, that from one

end of the country to the other everyone would know that something very wonderful had happened in the palace of the king.

The wrong man was out — and the right man was in!

10

Rejoice and Be Glad

ON THE VERY DAY THAT HAMAN HANGED, MORDECAI came before the king — "for Esther had told what he was unto her." Esther explained to King Ahasuerus that she belonged by adoption to Mordecai, who had intervened to save the king's life from the hand of the assassin; and that for the king to be identified with her must inevitably involve his identification with Mordecai, if there was to be harmony in his relationship to the queen.

In the light of all that had been revealed to him and with a profound sense of gratitude, not only for the preservation of his own life, but for his deliverance from the subtle, destructive influence of the enemy within the palace — "On that day did the king Ahasuerus give the house of Haman the Jews' enemy unto Esther the queen . . . and the king took off his ring, which he had taken from Haman, and gave it to Mordecai" (8:1, 2).

You will notice that the king did two things. He placed the ring upon Mordecai's finger, but he entrusted the administration of Haman's estate to Esther. In this way, although the king invested Mordecai with all the authority that once had belonged to Haman, this authority was to be exercised according to what Ahasuerus now considered to be the better judgment of Esther, the queen. Esther, for her part, indicated at once where she knew the better judgment lay; not in herself, but in Mordecai, whom she set over the house of Haman (8:2).

Thus the king identified his will with that of Esther, and Esther submitted her will to that of Mordecai, and I am sure that the spiritual significance of this new situation in the palace will be very obvious to you. When the soul, consisting of the mind, the emotions and the will (King Ahasuerus), is in total harmony with the desires created by the Holy Spirit (Mordecai) within a yielded human spirit (Esther) this is what the Bible describes as the "fulness of the Holy Ghost."

Allow me then to retrace our steps for a moment, so that we may get the overall picture in its full significance, recapitulating stage by stage.

THE HOLY SPIRIT RESISTED

This was the first picture, portrayed by the situation recorded in chapter three. Outside the palace Mordecai was sitting in the king's gate, while inside the palace Haman was plotting Mordecai's destruction, fearful lest Mordecai, who refused to bow in his presence, should gain access to the king and bring about that change of government which would introduce to the land those laws which Haman hated.

THE HOLY SPIRIT RECEIVED

Though bitterly opposed by Haman, as the Holy Spirit will always be bitterly opposed, resented and resisted by the flesh, chapter two spoke to us of the Holy Spirit coming into the human spirit, as Mordecai came into the life of Esther.

The basis was that of adoption, just as you and I must receive "the Spirit of Adoption," if we are to be born again into the family of forgiven sinners — "the Spirit itself bearing witness with our spirit, that we are the children of God" (Romans 8:15, 16).

The Holy Spirit Grieved

At the beginning of chapter four, Mordecai sat clothed in sackcloth and ashes, crying with a loud and bitter cry. This picture brought to us a vivid illustration of what happens when the Spirit of God is grieved.

Mordecai had come into the life of Esther and she ". . . did the commandments of Mordecai like as when she was brought up with him" (2:20), but Mordecai had not yet come into the life of the king. Haman still dominated the scene and projected his evil influence throughout the kingdom.

Here portrayed is the defeated Christian, described by Paul in his epistle to the Romans — "So you see how it is; my new life tells me to do right, but the old nature that is still inside me loves to sin. Oh, what a terrible thing this is! Who will free me from my slavery to this deadly lower nature?" (Romans 7:24, 25, *Living Letters*).

The Holy Spirit Quenched

This was the picture painted next, as chapter four continues. Esther was reluctant to obey Mordecai's instructions, and hesitated to go unsummoned into the presence of the king, thus to hazard her life in the interests of her people, that the seed of Abraham might not perish. Though his wickedness had been fully exposed to her, until Esther was prepared to die to her own ability to hang Haman, it was impossible for Mordecai to assume responsibility for putting this enemy into the place of death.

THE HOLY SPIRIT OBEYED

As it came to its climactic conclusion, the latter part of chapter four introduced us to the implications of true discipleship.

On the third morning Esther, as good as dead, entered into the royal presence, and the king held out the golden scepter. Losing her life, she found it again — to be identified forever with God's purpose, God's power, and God's people.

Thus the decks were cleared for those events recorded in chapters 5, 6 and 7 which would enlighten the understanding of the king — and bring Haman to the gallows!

THE FULLNESS OF THE HOLY SPIRIT

With the enemy deposed, and Mordecai with the king's ring upon his finger occupying his estate, and with the king and queen at one with each other in honoring Mordecai with all the executive powers of government, the stage had now been set for a new and glorious regime. That regime, which, when established spiritually within your soul, means that not only does the Lord Jesus Christ live by His Holy Spirit within your human spirit, but that He now controls your

mind, your emotions, and your will. By all that you
do and say and are, His life and likeness are expressed
through you.

People around you become aware of the fact —
though they may not understand it — that by the "ex-
ceeding great and precious promises" you have become
"partaker of the divine nature" (II Peter 1:4).

It is important to remember at this stage of the
story, that though Mordecai is welcome and at home
within the palace, he continues to communicate with
the king, through Esther the queen.

> "And Esther spake yet again before the king, and
> fell down at his feet, and besought him with tears
> to put away the mischief. . . .
> "And to reverse the letters devised by Haman
> the son of Hammedatha the Agagite, which he
> wrote to destroy the Jews which are in all the king's
> provinces" (8:3, 5).

This raises quite an interesting point. We have
already discussed in chapter 5 the duality of human
conscience — the moral conscience seated in the human
spirit, and the animal conscience seated in the human
soul. In the same way there appears to be a duality
in the exercise of the human will.

When you exercise your animal will, you make an
animal choice, governed by your animal conscience.
On the other hand, when you exercise your moral will,
you make a moral choice, governed by your moral conscience.

There is of course much that you do by the exercise of your animal will which has no moral significance, and your behavior then is king governed only

by your animal conscience; for your animal conscience simply decides what is consequentially right and what is consequentially wrong.

When a blazing log falls out of the fire, for instance, you decide not to pick it up with your hands, because that would be consequentially wrong — your hands would get burned! No moral issue, however, is involved in this decision. It is an animal choice which any sensible animal would make, faced with a comparable situation.

You walk by the exercise of your animal will the way a dog would walk — except that you only have two legs to do it with! You sit down, physically, the way a dog sits down, and you step into a car, physically, the way a dog steps into a car. That will which you exercise to bring the body into action to do these things is not morally involved.

The moral factor may well be introduced, however, if you are sitting down, when the work which you are paid to do demands that you should be standing up. Furthermore, though there may be no moral choice involved in the physical act of walking, there may well be a moral choice involved in the *direction* you have chosen to walk, and the company into which this will bring you.

Stepping into the car, starting the engine and driving down the road may demand no more than a series of physical acts with which your moral conscience and your moral will remain totally unconcerned, until you reach the main highway. There you have to decide whether to turn to the right or to the left. To turn to the right would take you to the club,

where, as an alcoholic you used to get drunk; to turn
to the left would take you home to your wife and family.

Even though you are born again, the sin principle
which still operates within you will seek to dominate
your animal will, so that you make the decisions which
will enable the flesh to use your body in order to realize
and satisfy its carnal appetites. At the same time it
will seek to silence your moral conscience, and to per-
suade your animal conscience that you can do it and
get away with it, without any unpleasant consequences.

Simultaneously, your moral conscience, quickened
and undergirded by the Holy Spirit within your human
spirit, will exercise its moral will to plead with your
animal will "to put away the mischief," saying in so
many words — "Do not let any part of your bodies become tools of wickedness, to be used for sinning; but
give yourselves completely to God — every part of you
— for you are back from death and you want to be
tools in the hands of God, to be used for His good
purposes" (Romans 6:13, *Living Letters*).

If the *flesh* is successful in silencing your moral
conscience and in exerting its influence over your animal will, you will turn right at the main highway, and
end up at the club — morally defeated. On the other
hand, if the Holy Spirit enables your *moral* will to exercise control over your animal will, you will turn left
and arrive home, to the delight of your wife and children, and to the inexpressible joy of your own soul —
morally victorious.

"But that's just it," you say, "right there when I
hit the highway, and have to make the choice — that's
where I run into trouble! That's where I am beaten

again and again! How can I get my animal will into harmony with my moral will? How, in my experience, can I get the ring on the right finger?" The answer lies in your attitude toward the Lord Jesus Christ, whose life you share.

When Esther went in once more before the king, and besought him with tears to put away the mischief and to reverse the letters, it was in an attitude of utter confidence in Mordecai. She felt certain that as her obedience to him had enabled Mordecai to put Haman into the place of death, so now her continued obedience to him would allow Mordecai to bring his gracious influence to bear upon the king's mind, and upon the decisions made in the palace.

As she once had died to her own ability to hang Haman, so she continued to die to her own ability to change the character of the king, for on this occasion too she entered, unsummoned, into his presence, and once more ". . . the king held out the golden sceptre toward Esther" (8:4). She was still living in the power of the third morning.

Resurrection life!

This too must be your attitude toward the Lord Jesus Christ. In every controversy between your moral will and the flesh, as to how your animal will is to be exercised in determining the things you think and say and do, you will say to him — "Dear Lord Jesus Christ, thank You for Your Holy Spirit to whom I yield my human spirit, and by whose gracious presence I share Your life, and share Your victory. I know that I cannot deal with the principle of sin within me, nor put the flesh into the place of death, but I thank You that You *can,* and that You *did,* when You died upon the cross, and I died with You. Thank You for Your Holy Spirit, who alone can make this real in my experience, mortifying those deeds of my body which have their origin in Satan. I am willing for You to invade my soul, to control my mind, to control my emotions, and to control my will, so that every decision within my soul will be in perfect harmony with my spirit; and my spirit in perfect harmony with You; so that my whole being may declare Your praise. Lord Jesus, I can't — but You can! Thank You so much!"

If you are prepared to practice the presence of Christ in this way, and reckon with Him through His Holy Spirit, not only to keep the flesh in the place of death, but to establish His divine sovereignty within every area of your soul, then you will experience that delightful transformation of character which will conform you increasingly to the image of God's dear Son. It will be a transformation characterized by all that happened throughout the land, once Mordecai was given the place of honor in the palace.

> "Then the king Ahasuerus said unto Esther the queen and to Mordecai the Jew, Behold, I have given Esther the house of Haman, and him they have hanged upon the gallows, because he laid his hand upon the Jews.
> "Write ye also for the Jews, as it liketh you, in the king's name, and seal it with the king's ring: for the writing which is written in the king's name, and sealed with the king's ring, may no man reverse. . . .
> "And it was written according to all that Mordecai commanded unto the Jews, and to the lieu-

tenants, and the deputies and rulers of the provinces which are from India unto Ethiopia, a hundred twenty and seven provinces, unto every province according to the writing thereof, and unto every people after their language, and to the Jews according to their writing, and according to their language.

"And he wrote in the king Ahasuerus' name, and sealed it with the king's ring . . . ." (8:7-10).

So the new edict was published; it was still in the name of the king, but no longer according to all that Haman commanded. It was now according to all that Mordecai commanded — "For Mordecai was great in the king's house, and his fame went out throughout all the provinces: for this man Mordecai waxed greater and greater" (9:4).

In the royal city of Shushan, throughout the king's provinces (9:16), in the villages and in the unwalled towns (9:19), all that had happened in the palace made a profound and lasting impact. There was no part of the community unaffected by the change, and everyone knew that something wonderful must have happened to the king.

As Mordecai established God's laws in the palace, so God's people, to whom these laws had been entrusted, had rest from their enemies (9:16). Sorrow was turned to joy, and mourning into a good day, while fear was replaced by fellowship, as they sent portions one to another and gave gifts to the poor (9:22).

Every new instruction, as Mordecai sent letters to all the Jews in the hundred twenty and seven provinces of the kingdom of King Ahasuerus, brought words of peace and truth (9:30).

Little wonder then that these days were to become days never to be forgotten in the history of this people. When the plot to destroy the Jews had been hatched in the wicked heart of Haman, a plot prompted by Satan's inherent hatred of the Promised Seed of faithful Abraham, Jesus Christ — Haman had cast lots according to an ancient custom called Pur, that he might select a lucky day on which to bring his evil designs to fruition.

The day chosen in this way was the thirteenth day of Adar, and on this one day, all Jews, both young and old, little children and women, were to perish (3:13).

Instead, far from perishing on the thirteenth day of the month, on the fourteenth day of Adar the Jews rejoiced with unspeakable joy, as a people wonderfully delivered. Sentenced to death, they had been raised from the dead, and the wicked device of Haman which he had devised against the Jews had returned upon his own head, that he and his sons should be hanged on the gallows (9:25). Years later, Satan's wicked device was to return upon *his* own wicked head, when the Lord Jesus, through death upon the cross, destroyed him who had the power of death, even the devil, and nailed *him* to his own gallows (Hebrews 2:14, 15).

So, year by year, throughout their generations, the Jewish people have celebrated the feast of Purim, named after Pur (by which custom Haman cast lots), in celebration of their great and gracious deliverance.

Another remarkable thing happened, too, for "many of the people of the land became Jews; for the fear of the Jews fell upon them" (8:17). They knew full well what had been destined for these people. Humanly speaking their situation had been hopeless — yet they had been snatched from the grave, and their enemies slain.

The people began to say to themselves — "If this is what it means to be numbered among the people of God, then I want to become a Jew. I want to know for myself the kind of God who can save His people from death, destroy their foes, and give them joy and peace and rest."

There is nothing quite so infectious as a man genuinely filled with the Holy Spirit!

True holiness is always evangelistic. It makes the sinner heartily sick of his sin, and causes him to hunger and thirst after righteousness, until he cries out from the depths of his soul — "Sirs, what must I do to be saved?" (Acts 16:30).

Is this the effect that *your* life has upon your neighbors, upon your workmates, upon your fellow-students, and upon your own children?

> "And Mordecai went out from the presence of the king in royal apparel of blue and white, and with a great crown of gold, and with a garment of fine linen and purple: and the city of Shushan rejoiced and was glad" (8:15).

How different everything had become. It seemed almost as if the sun shone brighter, and as though every cloud in the sky was laughing; the birds sang more sweetly and every flower had a new fragrance. The time had been when the king and Haman sat down to drink — Haman then was in the ascendency, and "the city of Shushan was perplexed." Now, with Haman on the gallows, and Mordecai in the palace, the "City Perplexed" had become the "City Rejoicing."

The psalmist knew something of this, I am sure, when inspired by the Holy Spirit he penned the 46th Psalm —

"God is our refuge and strength, a very present help in trouble.

"Therefore will not we fear . . . .

"There is a river, the streams whereof shall make glad the city of God, the holy place of the tabernacles of the most High.

"God is in the midst of her; she shall not be moved: God shall help her, and that right early . . .

"Be still, and know that I am God" (Psalm 46: 1, 2, 4, 5, 10).

This river has its source in the throne of God and of the Lamb (Revelation 22:1). It is the life of God in the soul of man — and the promise is to you and to your children! "He that believeth on me, as the scripture hath said, out of his belly [innermost being] shall flow rivers of living water. (But this spake he of the Spirit, which they that believe on him should receive; for the Holy Ghost was not yet given; because that Jesus was not yet glorified)" (John 7:38, 39).

Allow God so to strengthen you by His Spirit in the inner man, that the Lord Jesus may be glorified in your heart as He is glorified in heaven — then the river will flow, and make glad the city of God.

"Be filled with the Spirit; Speaking to yourselves in psalms and hymns and spiritual songs, singing and making melody in your heart to the Lord;

"Giving thanks always for all things unto God and the Father in the name of our Lord Jesus Christ" (Ephesians 5:19, 20).

Then you will have every right to rejoice and be glad!

11

The Privilege of Being You

NEVER BREAK YOUR HEART TRYING TO BE SOMEONE ELSE!

In the first place, you never will be! You will always be *you*, and no one else. The person who gets up in the morning will be the person who went to bed the night before; so you might as well get reconciled to the fact that *you* are the person you are going to live with for the rest of your days.

In the second place, it is the way God wants it! He never intended that you should be anyone else but *you* — but what He *would* like, is that you should learn how to be the person He intended you to be.

King Ahasuerus was a different person at the beginning of the story of the Book of Esther, from the King Ahasuerus at the end of the story. It is important to bear in mind however, that it was the same king — the same mind, the same emotions, and the same will.

Had Ahasuerus continued to behave under the influence of Haman, and had he continued to identify himself with Haman's wicked ways, he would have been responsible for one of the cruelest massacres in human history. His name would have gone down in ignominy and shame. As it was, under the influence of Mordecai and identified with *his* gracious ways, the king earned the honor and respect of a happy and a prosperous people. If others were astonished at the change, maybe there were none more astonished than the king himself!

Ahasuerus had learned the difference between the man that Haman could make of him — the "old man" — and the man that Mordecai could make of him — the "new man." He had come under entirely new management!

This may help you to understand what the Lord Jesus Christ meant, in what might otherwise appear to have been a contradiction, when on one occasion He said to His disciples — "If any man will come after me, let him deny himself, and take up his cross, and follow me" (Matthew 16:24). It becomes quite evident from this statement that there is a self to be denied — that is to say —

A SELF TO BE REPUDIATED

On another occasion however, when a certain lawyer stood up and tempted Him, saying — "Master, what shall I do to inherit eternal life?" — the Lord Jesus Christ replied by quoting the law from the sixth chapter of the Book of Deuteronomy — "Thou shalt love the Lord thy God with all thy heart, and with all thy soul, and with all thy strength, and with all thy mind; and thy neighbour as thyself" (Luke 10:25-27).

If you are to love your neighbor *as yourself*, then you must first love yourself; otherwise on this basis, love for your neighbor would become meaningless. It would appear therefore, from the answer given by the Lord Jesus to those who questioned Him, that there is a legitimate place for self-love, and that in addition to a self to be repudiated, there must be

A SELF TO BE RESPECTED

How then is self-respect to be reconciled with self-repudiation? Can they be coexistent?

The answer to this problem is clearly illustrated in the person of King Ahasuerus. He had to repudiate the kind of man that Haman made of him, but he had the right to respect the kind of man that Mordecai made of him. In the same way, the self that you have to repudiate, is the self that the flesh makes of you when the flesh is dominant within the soul — *abusing* and *misusing* your personality. The self, however, that you have the right to respect, is the self that Christ makes of you — filling you with His Holy Spirit, *enhancing* and *using* your personality.

> "I (*the self that sin makes of me*) am crucified with Christ; nevertheless I live (*the self that Christ makes of me*); yet not I, but Christ liveth in me" (Galatians 2:20).

This is the *you* which God wants you to become, for this is the *you* which God intended you to be.

There is most certainly a legitimate place for healthy self-respect in your life as a Christian, but it is the self-respect that derives from your personal relationship to Jesus Christ.

On this basis you can learn to love the most unlovely of your neighbors, because you know that if there is anything that you can love or respect about yourself, it is only what Christ has made of you. So though your neighbor lies drunken in the gutter, you can love him. Not for the man that sin has made of him, but for the man you know that Christ can make of him, once He has taken over — for what He has made of you, He can make of him!

You do not lose your own personality when you take your place by faith with Christ in death. On the contrary, a transformation takes place *within* your personality. *You* simply come under new management, so that "When someone becomes a Christian he becomes a brand new person inside. He is not the same any more. A new life has begun! All these new things are from God Who brought us back to Himself through what Christ Jesus did" (II Corinthians 5:17, 18, *Living Letters*).

The new life which has begun, of course, is the life of the Lord Jesus, and your personality becomes His means of expression. It is He who, as God, works through you, "both to will and to do of His good pleasure" (Philippians 2:13). When you are prepared for the Lord Jesus Christ really to get into business like that, you will not *want* to be anyone else!

You will be far too excited discovering what He intends *you* to be!

It was no good for Jacob to try to inherit the promises, because that was the man the flesh made of him; God had prepared the inheritance for *Israel* — the man that *only God* could make of Jacob.

It was no good for Simon to try to be an apostle, for that was the man the flesh made of him; God had called *Peter* — the man that *only God* could make of Simon.

It was no good for Saul of Tarsus to try to defend the faith, for that was the man the flesh made of him; God wanted *Paul the Apostle,* and that was the man that *only God* could make of Saul of Tarsus.

Has God changed *your* name yet?

Did you ever give Him the chance?

God changes the *name* when God changes the *man!*

THE TEN SONS OF HAMAN

I wonder if, as you have been reading these pages, some such thoughts as these have been passing through your mind — "I understand the picture quite clearly. Just as Haman was hanged upon the gallows, so in the purpose of God my old sinful nature was nailed to the cross with the Lord Jesus Christ — executed and buried. Now that Haman is hanged, however, is that the last that will ever be heard of him?

"Does this mean that my old, sinful nature is wholly eradicated the moment I claim by faith my identity with Christ in death? Is the new Israel that Christ creates in me, never to be troubled again by the old Jacob; and is Peter never again to be confronted by Simon?"

If this is what you have been thinking, then these are good questions, and I believe the answer is to be found quite easily — illustrated for us in a fascinating way, in the ninth chapter of the Book of Esther.

"Then said Esther, If it please the king, let it be granted to the Jews which are in Shushan to do to-

morrow also according unto this day's decree, and
let Haman's ten sons be hanged upon the gallows.

"And the king commanded it so to be done: and
the decree was given at Shushan; and they hanged
Haman's ten sons" (9:13, 14).

That's the answer! Haman had ten sons!

You may die today to your own ability to put Haman into the place of death, thus allowing the Holy
Spirit to celebrate in you the victory of the Lord Jesus,
putting Haman on the cross — but this will not do for
tomorrow! You will discover that Haman has ten sons.
That is not all, for the Haman of your own heart not
only has ten sons, but every one of these ten sons has
ten sons more!

There is no climactic experience by which the evil
influence of the flesh may be eradicated once and for
all, though the flesh itself in its subtilty would like you
to believe it — in the interests of its own self-preserva-
tion! Only be persuaded that the flesh no longer exists,
and you are not likely to cause it any further incon-
venience as it perpetuates its wicked activities in your
soul. Nothing could please the devil more than that!

Appropriation of the victory of Christ demands
more than just one *act* of faith — it requires an *attitude*
of faith. It is a moment-by-moment reckoning, and your
reckoning for this moment is never adequate for the
next. "Walk in the spirit, and ye shall not fulfil the
lusts of the flesh. For the flesh lusteth against the
Spirit, and the Spirit against the flesh" (Galatians 5:
16, 17).

Walking in the Spirit is a continuous process, one
step at a time. It means that for every new situation

into which every new step brings you, you must reckon positively with the Holy Spirit, to keep the flesh in the place of death.

I want to emphasize the need to reckon *positively*, for we are not only to reckon ourselves "to be dead indeed unto sin," but we are to reckon ourselves "alive unto God through Jesus Christ our Lord" (Romans 6:11). It is our enjoyment of the resurrection life of the Lord Jesus Christ, through reckoning positively with His presence, which sets us free from the law of sin and death. The surest way of reckoning yourself to be dead to sin (that old Adamic nature), is to reckon yourself alive in Jesus Christ and be utterly dependent upon Him. He then will take care of the consequences.

Quite obviously, by the statement Paul made in the epistle to the Galatians, he recognized that the flesh is still active in the believer. If to walk in the Spirit is not to fulfill the lusts of the flesh, then the converse would be equally true. *Not* to walk in the Spirit — that is to say, to walk other than in moment-by-moment dependence upon Him — means that you will fall prey to the lusts of the flesh, and encounter to your discomfort some of Haman's many sons and grandsons — the evil progeny of Amalek.

Israel will encounter Jacob; Peter will behave like Simon, and Paul will have a brush with Saul of Tarsus.

The Bible presents an overwhelming case for Christian victory, as long as we are prepared to fulfill the conditions and appropriate by faith the victorious life of Christ Himself. On the other hand, nowhere in the Bible is there any support for the promise of sinless perfection, save on that wonderful day when we shall see the Lord Jesus Christ face to face. Then indeed "we shall be like him, for we shall see him as he is" (I John 3:2).

Do not allow anyone, therefore, to deceive you, for this will only lead you into dishonesty, no matter how sincere you may be, as you seek to reconcile a bad conscience with your claim to sinless perfection. You will simply have to invent some other name for sin and pretend that it does not exist.

The Holy Spirit is your Comforter and Friend; He is within you to keep you from falling, but be very sensitive to what He has to say to you —

> "For the Lord corrects *and* disciplines every one whom He loves, and He punishes, even scourges, every son whom He accepts *and* welcomes to His heart *and* cherishes.
>
> "You must submit to *and* endure [correction] for discipline. God is dealing with you as with sons; for what son is there whom his father does not [thus] train *and* correct *and* discipline?
>
> "Now if you are exempt from correction *and* left without discipline in which all [of God's children] share, then you are illegitimate offspring *and* not true sons [at all]" (Hebrews 12:6-8, *Amplified Bible*).

In other words, when the Holy Spirit names it — call it by its name! Admit and confess it for the sin that it is. Claim instantly the cleansing that God has promised through the blood of Christ, and be thankful that the Greater Mordecai (the Holy Spirit) is in residence — constantly alert, and ready instantly to expose the wickedness of Haman's breed, and to save you from the evil.

THE POWER OF VETO AND THE MORAL CHOICE

"For Mordecai the Jew was next unto king Ahasuerus, and great among the Jews, and accepted of the multitude of his brethren, seeking the wealth of his people, and speaking peace to all his seed" (10:3).

If you have received the Lord Jesus Christ as your Saviour, then you have become a child of God, and it will be the constant delight of the Holy Spirit to seek your wealth and welfare, and to speak peace to your soul. One thing may have struck you however, in this last verse of the last chapter. "Mordecai the Jew," it is stated, "was next unto king Ahasuerus."

You will remember from an earlier chapter, that when Pharaoh placed the ring upon Joseph's finger, as King Ahasuerus now had placed the ring upon that of Mordecai, he retained his sovereignty and the power of veto. He said — "Only in the throne will I be greater than thou." Joseph was next unto Pharaoh, as Mordecai was next unto the king.

This is a most important lesson to learn, for the amazing fact is this — that in His relationship to man God has limited Himself, in spite of His omnipotence, by the law of faith.

Though the Holy Spirit inhabits your humanity as God, representing in His Person both the Father and the Son as God, He will never violate the sovereignty of your will, nor deprive you of the moral responsibility to choose.

Though God Himself, He has chosen always to be "next" within the kingdom of your soul, and if He is to govern your behavior and exercise supreme control in every part of your being, it will only ever be by your own free choice and glad consent.

It is this power of veto — this right to choose — which lifts you out of the animal kingdom, and makes you the moral being that God created man to be. It is this, and only this, which enables you to love God back, and so reciprocate His love for you.

That is why your free "yes" to God, at any given moment, fills His heart with greater joy than all the thrilling wonders of a million universes, thrown out into the vastness of outer space by the word of His power. They have no capacity to love Him — because they have no capacity to choose Him!

The privilege of being *you* is that you can know God and love God — *for yourself!*

12

Pig Is Pig

King Ahasuerus had made a wonderful discovery.

He had discovered that the evil of which he was capable under the influence of Haman, could be matched only by the good of which he was capable under the influence of Mordecai. It is this same wonderful discovery which God wants you to make, for it is absolutely basic to an intelligent understanding of the Christian life.

This discovery is not only charged with comfort and encouragement for your soul, but is calculated to deliver you from the heartbreak, frustration and despair which is the unhappy lot of so many sincere Christians, in their earnest endeavors to please God in the energy of the flesh.

The remarkable change that took place in the character of the king did not come about by improving Haman, but by replacing him with Mordecai. It was not a question of reformation, but of substitution — an exchanged life.

Haman was rotten through and through, a master

of duplicity, and he never changed. There was no re-
deeming feature about him, and he was entirely without remedy; fit only to die upon his own gallows.

This is exactly what God has to say about that old
Adamic nature within you, called the flesh, and this
was Paul's persuasion — "I know I am rotten through
and through so far as my old sinful nature is concerned"
(Romans 7:18, *Living Letters*). It is absolutely im-
perative for your own spiritual well-being that you
recognize the fact that this old nature will never change
its character. All the wickedness of which it is capable
today, it will be capable of tomorrow — or for that
matter fifty years from now. The flesh within you then
will be as wicked as the flesh within you today, and
there is absolutely no salvageable content within it.

What a relief it must be for you to discover that in
all your attempts to harness the flesh in the service of
Jesus Christ, and in all your painful endeavors to introduce it to godly principles of life and conduct, God
has never expected anything of you but the hopeless
failure you have been!

You have been trying to do the impossible!

The Christians in the Galatian church had made
the same mistake, for they had been trying to achieve
holiness in their own strength. They tried to submit
themselves to rules and regulations imposed upon them
by Judaistic legalists, who gloried in their conformity
to Jewish custom. Outward form and ritualistic pattern
had become a substitute for the spontaneous expression
of the indwelling life of Christ.

"O you poor *and* silly *and* thoughtless *and* unreflecting *and* senseless Galatians! . . . .

"Let me ask you this one question: Did you receive the (Holy) Spirit as the result of obeying the Law *and* doing its works, or was it by hearing [the message of the Gospel] and believing [it]? . . . .

"Are you so foolish *and* so senseless *and* so silly? Having begun [your new life spiritually] with the (Holy) Spirit, are you now reaching perfection [by dependence] on the flesh?" (Galatians 3:1-3, *Amplified Bible*).

My home is at Capernwray Hall, which is a Conference Grounds and Bible School, just south of the Lake District in a very beautiful part of Northern England. Although my ministry in different parts of the world involves long periods of separation from my family, that is where I live with my wife and four boys. Perhaps you have an imagination vivid enough to suppose with me, for a moment, that I have decided to embark upon a certain experiment.

Imagine, if you will, that I have come to the conclusion that the pig as a species has been grossly misjudged; that the idea that a pig wallows in the muck by choice, and that by nature it loves the dirt, is wholly unfounded. I have become fully persuaded that it is a question purely of environment, education and upbringing!

I decide, therefore, to adopt a little baby pig into the family, and in this way prove my point by offering to it those amenities of life which will enable the best side of its character to be developed. Of course I explain my plans to my wife, and calling my sons to a family conference, say to them — "Now, boys, I want to have your co-operation in a little experiment in which I am engaging. We are adopting this little pig, and I want you to treat it with great kindness and to receive it into the family just like one of yourselves."

We give the little pig a pink satin shirt and some little blue velvet pants, with ivory buttons down the sides. We teach it to wipe its feet when it comes into the house, to sit up at the table, to bow its head when we say grace, and to sleep at night between the sheets and the blankets with which we provide it, in its own little bed.

Mind you, I can't say that the pig shows any particular enthusiasm about the experiment, and it appears to be somewhat bewildered at all the strange things that are happening. However, it decides to go along with the idea, and in spite of all the many set-backs and somewhat feeble co-operation on the part of the pig, after some months it would appear that there are solid grounds for encouragement. In fact, we are getting quite excited, and even some of the neighbors — who, quite frankly, had viewed our experiment with considerable skepticism — are now becoming increasingly impressed by the progress that we have made.

It becomes quite obvious to us that it is only a matter of time before our endeavors are crowned with success. Unfortunately, it is just at this juncture, when our hopes are running high, that we make one fatal blunder.

Somebody leaves the door open that leads into the grounds!

Fresh breezes blow into the room where the little pig is playing. Sensing the fragrance of new-mown hay, the little pig's nose begins to twitch. Stopping halfway across the room it gazes out into the park—its curly tail unwinds and shoots straight up, stiff as a rod — like an aerial! There is a moment of hesitation, and then suddenly — like a bullet from a gun — the little pig races out through the open door and across the park, moving at incredible speed!

Reaching the muddiest bog it can find, the little pig plunges in, and after rolling over and over, it lies on its back in the mud, little blue pants and all. With a delightful grin on its face, and with its feet sticking up in the air, it cries at the top of its voice — "Home, sweet home!"

You see, change its environment as you will, and train it as you may — little pink pants or blue, satin shirt or clean straw — *Pig Is Pig!*

Given half a chance, the nature of the beast is to get back to where it belongs, and this you have found to be true in your *own* experience. The flesh within you has never ceased to love sin, and never will. Given half a chance it, too, will want to get back to where it belongs and wallow in the muck!

This is why the godliest of men still have latent within them the most terrible potential for evil. It is the godliest of men who know it best, for it is the acknowledgment of this very fact which is the secret of their godliness. They have learned long since, with King Ahasuerus, and often by bitter experience, that character does not change for the better by improving the flesh, but by allowing it to be replaced by the Holy Spirit — for pig is pig! Only the Holy Spirit can render its pernicious appetites inoperative.

Abraham discovered this when he went down into Egypt and lied to Pharaoh. (See Genesis 12.) Moses discovered this when it went ill with him for the sake of the Israelites who so provoked his spirit, "that he spake unadvisedly with his lips." (See Numbers 20 and Psalm 106:32, 33.) Samson discovered this in the arms of Delilah, and "he wist not that the Lord was departed from him." (See Judges 17.) David discovered this when he sent Uriah to his death and committed adultery with Bath-sheba. (See II Samuel 11.) Peter discovered this when he denied Christ to His face and went out and "wept bitterly." (See Luke 22.)

Paul reminds us that this is what happened to Israel. God never intended to *improve their lot* under Pharaoh, but to *exchange their land*. God intended to substitute Canaan for Egypt, and in an exchanged land introduce His people to an exchanged life.

Believing God enough to get out, Israel did not believe God enough to get in. Instead, they sought to establish a new way of life in the wilderness and experienced nothing of the good things which God had provided for them in the Land of Promise. Little wonder, therefore, that their new life in the wilderness was thoroughly contaminated by those appetites which could only be satisfied in Egypt; and they constantly wanted to get back to where those appetites belonged.

In this context Paul wrote to the Christians in Corinth, of whom this was so singularly true, and who

evidenced so much of carnality in their behavior and
in their practice of the Christian faith —

> "All these things happened to them as examples,
> as object lessons to us, to warn us against doing the
> same things; they were written down so that we
> could read about them and learn from them in
> these last days as the world nears its end.
>
> "So be careful. If you are thinking, 'Oh, I would
> never behave like that' — let this be a warning to
> you. For you too may fall into sin.
>
> "But remember this, the wrong desires that come
> into your life are not new and different. Many
> others have faced exactly the same problems before
> you. And you can trust God to keep temptation
> from becoming so strong that you can't stand up
> against it, for He has promised this and He will do
> what He says. He will show you how to escape
> temptation's power so that you can bear up patient-
> ly against it" (I Corinthians 10:11-13, *Living Let-
> ters*).

Be persuaded, therefore, of the wickedness of your
own heart, and humbly confess it before God. Never
be shocked nor dismayed at the amazing capacity for
sin that lies within you, for this is the nature of your
case.

It is only when you are honest enough to face up
to these facts, that you will have, on the one hand, a
big enough view of what the Lord Jesus Christ came
into the world to do for you; and on the other hand,
the desire to let Him do it!

The Lord Jesus Christ wants so very much to replace, by His Presence within you, all your inherent
potential for evil under the influence of the flesh. He

offers you instead all His limitless potential for good, through the energy and power of His Holy Spirit.

This can never be accomplished by putting Haman through the beauty parlor! It is the gallows he needs — with the ring off his finger and the rope around his neck!

13

The Conclusion of the Matter

SPIRITUAL NEW BIRTH INVOLVES THE PRINCIPLE OF DIVINE substitution, and though you are to be persuaded of your inherent wickedness, you are to be equally persuaded of Christ's inherent righteousness. If that which is born of the flesh is flesh — and pig is pig — you can be equally certain that that which is born of the Spirit is Spirit — and God is God!

What is so completely amazing is that God is prepared to be God in you; not figuratively, but factually! You can share His life and be transformed into His likeness — "For as you know Him better, He will give you, through His great power, everything you need for living a truly good life: He even shares His own glory and His own goodness with us! And by that same mighty power He has given us all the other rich and wonderful blessings He promised; for instance, the promise to save us from the lust and rottenness all around us, and to give us His own character" (II Peter 1:3, 4, *Living Letters*).

This is the main thrust of what John has to say in his first epistle:

"He that committeth sin is of the devil; for the devil sinneth from the beginning. For this purpose the Son of God was manifested, that he might destroy the works of the devil.

"Whosoever is born of God doth not commit sin; for his seed remaineth in him: and he cannot sin, because he is born of God" (I John 3:8, 9).

Every act of sin has its origin in Satan; it is his character incarnate. It is what Haman makes of you when Haman wears the ring.

Evey act of righteousness has its origin in God; it is His character incarnate. It is what Mordecai makes of you when Mordecai wears the ring.

It is in the author of the act that its true character may be discerned. It is not a question of pattern, but of parentage — "In this the children of God are manifest, and the children of the devil" (I John 3:10). It was to bring about a change of authorship that the Son of God was manifested, "That he might destroy the works of the devil."

The Lord Jesus Christ came to get the wrong man out and the right man in!

When the Lord Jesus Christ died upon the cross He not only paid the price of your redemption, He put the rope around Haman's neck. He then rose again from the dead and ascended to the Father, that He might come, according to His promise, and take up residence within you — to live again on earth, but clothed with your humanity.

That which is born of God in you is Jesus Christ, and it is He who does not commit sin, nor *can* He — for God is God! This is what John means when he says,

". . . for his seed remaineth in him." It is the divine seed. It is the very nature of God Himself, and the nature that He wants to share with you through His Son.

Share the nature of Christ and you share His victory. You do not *achieve* it — you receive it; for Christ is made unto us "wisdom, and righteousness, and sanctification, and redemption: That, according as it is written, He that glorieth, let him glory in the Lord" — and "That no flesh should glory in his presence" (I Corinthians 1:29-31).

It was the crucified Lord Jesus who put the noose around Haman's neck; but if in your experience Haman is to be hoisted on his own scaffold, then you need the risen, living Lord Jesus at the other end of the rope. It is He alone who, by His Holy Spirit, the Greater Mordecai, can put him and keep him where he belongs. You cannot carry out the execution, but to you, and to you alone belongs the moral responsibility of confirming sentence of death.

Limited in His sovereignty by that law of faith which gives to you the moral capacity to know Him and to love Him for yourself, this is the decision which God is waiting for you to make.

Consent to die to all that you are which does not derive from all that Christ is, and thank Him for His willingness to make it real in your experience. Then you too will be able to say — "Now I really realize that not only am I in Christ, but that Christ is in me — I also realize that there is no further basic issue to face!"

You will have come to know God in a new and a thrilling way for yourself. Life will have become the adventure God intended it to be, and though a thousand Haman's may beset you, dead to yourself and alive to God, you will share the life of Jesus Christ and you will share His victory.

You will also share His compassion for the lost, and become expendable for God in the service of mankind. To know Christ more fully, and to make Him known will become the consuming passion of your soul.

"We rest on Thee" — our Shield and our Defender!
We go not forth alone against the foe;
Strong in Thy strength, safe in Thy keeping tender,
"We rest on Thee, and in Thy Name we go."

Yes, "in Thy Name," O Captain of salvation!
In Thy dear Name, all other names above;
Jesus our Righteousness, our sure Foundation,
Our Prince of glory and our King of love.

We go in faith, our own great weakness feeling,
And needing more each day Thy grace to know:
Yet from our hearts a song of triumph pealing;
"We rest on Thee, and in Thy Name we go."

"We rest on Thee" — our Shield and our Defender!
Thine is the battle, Thine shall be the praise,
When passing through the gates of pearly splendour,
Victors — we rest *with* Thee, through endless days.

— *Edith Gilling Cherry*

In the face of death itself, that duty might be done, you will echo with Esther of old — "If I perish, I perish! God take the consequences!"

And He will!